God's Living Water

COVERED IN JESUS' GRACE

Devotional

CONCORDIA PUBLISHING HOUSE · SAINT LOUIS

Copyright © 2022 Concordia Publishing House
3558 S. Jefferson Avenue, St. Louis, MO 63118-3968
1-800-325-3040 • cph.org

Scripture quotations are from the ESV® Bible (The Holy Bible, English Standard Version®), copyright © 2001 by Crossway, a publishing ministry of Good News Publishers. Used by permission. All rights reserved.

Manufactured in the United States of America

1   2   3   4   5   6   7   8   9   10   31   30   29   28   27   26   25   24   23   22

TABLE OF CONTENTS

God Creates All Creatures

~~~~~~~~~

Water is everywhere. We are surrounded by it; we are dependent on it. It falls from the sky in rain and runs through our landscapes in rivers. Water nourishes the trees, the plants, and our crops. The majority of the earth is covered in water, and that water is teeming with life and mystery. Without water, there would be no life on earth. Without water, we die. With water, we live and are satisfied.

God's Living Water: Covered in Jesus' Grace is a series that will take us on a journey through God's epic plan of salvation in the Bible. As we go, we will stop along the way and investigate some of the ways water is used and depicted in Scripture. As you read and meditate on these Scripture passages, the image of water as both a tool of God and a metaphor for His work will continually unfold for you.

Let us begin at the beginning. In Genesis 1, God created the heavens and the earth. Before God differentiated earth's various spaces and created life, the earth was formless. We learn from Genesis 1:2 and 2 Peter 3:5 that God sculpted His creation in six days from a watery chaos. God took this formless mass He had made and created order. He separated the waters into oceans and atmosphere. He filled the waters with creatures at His command and filled the earth with vegetation and animal life that fed off those waters. He made His special creation, Adam and Eve, the first man and woman, and placed them in a special garden. This Eden was fed by the waters of four rivers. Out of the watery deep, God formed and created order in His creation.

God's special creation, man and woman, were tempted by a demon, the fallen angel Satan, to defy God's laws. They joined in Satan's rebellion and were cast out of that perfect paradise. Yet God promised that a descendant of those first humans would crush Satan's power, reversing what had been done. Though God's people would remain in exile from Eden, they looked forward to the day when paradise would be restored to them. On the cross, Jesus, the Promised One, crushed Satan's power. In Him, God's people have the forgiveness of sins and those who have faith in Him are reconciled to God. We look forward to the day when Jesus returns in glory and paradise is restored in the new creation for God's people.

In this week's Scripture readings and devotional meditations, we'll investigate how God uses water to create order and restoration for His people. Just as He formed the waters of that creation to achieve His will, He worked throughout His plan of salvation to preserve and order His people.

God's Promised Land

Read Deuteronomy 11:1–17.

After Adam and Eve sinned against God, He cast them out of paradise. In the fallen world, the ground would no longer work to their advantage. Instead, they would have to struggle against the thorns, weeds, and environment to produce crops to survive. Whereas in Eden the waters of the four rivers fed and nourished the ground, in the broken world water would be an unpredictable commodity.

Throughout the centuries after Adam and Eve, God's people experienced many hardships and trials. Yet through them all, God was with them and never abandoned them. One of the central events of the lives of God's people, in which God worked mighty miracles and wonders, was the exodus. God's people had been enslaved in Egypt. Through His servant Moses, God freed His people from bondage and led them to the Promised Land. He led them through the Red Sea and destroyed the Egyptian army that pursued them. On their way from miserable slavery in Egypt to the land that would one day be Israel, God's people endured forty years of wandering in the wilderness in and around the Sinai Peninsula. In this harsh land, God refined His people. They depended on Him for daily bread, water, and protection. More often than not, these provisions came through miracles and wonders. An entire generation grew up as nomads in a harsh, dry, wilderness landscape, living in tents and learning to trust in God for all things. At the end of those forty years, God led them to the edge of their Promised Land. Through Moses, God reminded them of His covenant with them and commanded them to remain faithful to Him as they transitioned from wilderness wanderings to their new home. Moses said,

> But the land you are going over to possess is a land of hills and valleys, which drinks water by the rain from heaven, a land that the LORD your God cares for. The eyes of the LORD your God are always upon it, from the beginning of the year to the end of the year.
>
> And if you will obey my commandments that I command you today, to love the LORD your God, and to serve Him with all your heart and with all your soul, He will give the rain for your land in its season, the early rain and the later rain, that you may gather in your grain and your wine and your oil. And He will give grass in your fields for your livestock, and you shall eat and be full. (DEUTERONOMY 11:11–15)

In this picture of bondage, wilderness wanderings, and a promised land, we catch a glimpse of the Christian life. In Christ, God has freed us from the powers of sin, death, and the devil. In Baptism, like in the Red Sea, God delivered us from our bondage to Satan and crushed His power over us by the forgiveness of sins. He likewise has promised us an abundant future, the promised land of the new creation, where there will be no more sin and death. Moses promised God's people a temporal land abundant with rain and rivers that would nourish them. Jesus has promised His people a new eternal creation where we will be eternally satisfied and nourished by the Living Water.

In the wilderness wanderings of our lives, we look forward to that promised land of the new creation. It is not ours yet. In the meantime, just like with God's people in the wilderness, God works to care for and continually refine us. He provides for us and guides us by His Word. He nourishes us and sustains us with the bread of life in the Sacraments. He is with us in the dry times of life, sustaining us with His gifts through the parched land of this broken creation. He will lead His chosen and redeemed people to the promised land of the new creation. There we will never hunger or thirst again.

Thanksgiving for God's Care

Read Psalm 95.

It is easy to look at the world around us and see only the chaos. Besides the chaos brought about by human evil and destruction, there is also the chaos of the broken natural world. We read of earthquakes, fires, pandemics, and tornadoes. Much of the chaos in the world is brought about by water or lack thereof. We hear of famines, droughts, and floods. In the midst of so much visible chaos and destruction, it is easy to give into the temptation that God is not present in the world, acting in creation. We ask, If God could stop so much pain and suffering in the world, why doesn't He?

We turn to the Psalms to read God's truth on the matter. In Psalm 95, the psalmist, likely David, sang a song of thanks and praise to God. In it, the psalmist acknowledged God's hand in all of creation, how He orders the chaos of the natural world and has a hand in all its workings. He wrote,

> **The LORD is a great God, and a great King above all gods. In His hand are the depths of the earth; the heights of the mountains are His also. The sea is His, for He made it, and His hands formed the dry land.** (PSALM 95:3–5)

The psalmist did not write this song of praise from a place of comfort or ignorance. There can be no doubt that the suffering he experienced in the ancient world through sickness, pain, death, and other natural disasters dwarfs our modern experiences. Yet even in the midst of so much seeming chaos in the natural world, the psalmist acknowledged that God is still in control. Though the works of God seem unclear and shrouded in mystery, He is not absent from His creation.

The reality is that we do not know why God specifically allows certain disasters to occur. That is typically not for us to know. When confronted with the brokenness in the world we cannot understand, we often question God, demanding to know why He permits what we perceive as evil. The better question, however, is to follow the psalmist's example and ask who God is and what He does for us. In the midst of so much we do not understand, we look to Scripture and see the triune God. He who created all things out of nothing, who formed creation out of watery chaos, did not abandon it in its brokenness. Instead, the Father sent the Son, who died on the cross and rose again, to restore humanity to Himself. The Father and the Son send the Spirit to us, through Word and Sacrament, using water in Holy Baptism to cleanse us of our sins before God.

This is who our God is. He is still God in the midst of drought, famine, and flood. He still watches over and cares for His creation, and He will not abandon it to its brokenness. Instead, He is preparing a new promised land, the new creation, for His people redeemed by Christ. In light of God's ongoing care for His creation now, and looking forward to the new creation that He has promised us, with the psalmist we, too, can proclaim,

> **Oh come, let us worship and bow down; let us kneel before the Lord, our Maker! For He is our God, and we are the people of His pasture, and the sheep of His hand.** (Psalm 95:6–7)

God's Covenant of Peace

Read Ezekiel 34:25–30.

Throughout God's epic plan of salvation as described in Scripture, God's people continually turned away from true faith in Him. And while they deserved nothing from God, He remained patient with them. In His mercy, God sent prophets to serve as His mouthpiece to speak His truth to wandering hearts. Through these prophets, God continually called people to repent of their sins, receive forgiveness, and return to Him.

Nowhere in Scripture were more prophets sent in a shorter time span than in the years immediately before and during the time of the exile. After Moses had led the people to the Promised Land, God's people settled down, driving out the inhabitants and moving into their cities. They were brought out of the dry, harsh wilderness to the rains and rivers of the Promised Land. Yet they failed to remove the influence of the false demonic gods and idols that had infected the land. God's people continually turned away from true worship, forgot God's promises, and did evil. For centuries, God called and sent prophet after prophet to His people. For centuries, He called them to repentance to receive forgiveness. Sometimes they heard God's message and repented, other times they did not. As the sins of His people became more grievous, God sent more and more of His prophets to warn the people to turn from their sins and return to God.

Eventually, after either refusing to listen to or killing God's prophets, the consequences of the sins of God's people crashed down on them. God sent invading armies, first from Assyria in the north and then from Babylon, to bring His just punishment upon His people. Many died in the invasions, many were brought into exile hundreds of miles away in foreign lands. To so many, it would seem that God had abandoned them in their sins. God took away the lush Promised Land, and once again God's people were sent into the wilderness—not a desert wilderness but foreign lands ruled by emperors who neither knew nor feared the God of creation.

But even then, while His people were in exile and experiencing other great distress, God sent His prophets. One was Ezekiel, who lived in exile in Babylon. As God's people cried out to God, living the terrible consequences of their sins in a foreign land, Ezekiel communicated God's truth to them. Among his often enigmatic writings, Ezekiel prophesied hope. Inspired by the Holy Spirit, Ezekiel wrote,

> **And I will make them and the places all around My hill a blessing, and I will send down the showers in their season; they shall be showers of blessing. And the trees of the field shall yield their fruit, and the earth shall yield its increase, and they shall be secure in their land. And they shall know that I am the LORD, when I break the bars of their yoke, and deliver them from the hand of those who enslaved them.**
> (EZEKIEL 34:26–27)

This prophecy foretold God returning His exiled people to the Promised Land. At the same time, it pointed to something much greater that would happen hundreds of years after the people returned. It pointed to the coming Messiah, Jesus Christ, who would break the bars of sin, death, and hell that enslaved God's people. On the cross, Jesus did just that, and by rising to new life, Jesus secured a new promised land, the new creation, for all who believe in Him. There, the showers will not just be nourishing rain showers but also showers of blessing for eternity. There will no longer be need for prophets to communicate God's truth to us, as God will be in our very presence, and all suffering and death will be no more. Once again, God will bring order out of the apparent chaos of the world.

God Continually Provides

Read Luke 12:22–34.

As children, we often had our needs provided by others. Though we may have had jobs and responsibilities, in our childhood and youth, we did not have to pay our own way through life. We did not have to work to pay rent, we did not have to budget and pay bills, we did not have to make and keep routine health appointments, and we did not have to file taxes. As we grow up and become more independent, however, we must learn to do these things on our own. The process of learning to adjust to adult life in society can be jarring, confusing, and depressing. Frankly, adulthood never stops throwing new experiences and unfamiliar situations at us.

Central to being an adult is dealing with anxiety and insecurity about the unknown. Life is challenging and expensive. There is always one more expense on the horizon, there is always one more thing that goes wrong. There is just so much that can go wrong and so much to be anxious about. As long as the world is broken by suffering and sin, work and life will challenge and often disappoint us.

It was into this reality that God the Father sent His Son. Jesus was born into human flesh. He walked among the broken and anxious. He taught the struggling. He healed the suffering. In His great compassion, the very God who was there at the beginning of all things entered into His creation. The One who created divine order out of the chaos of the formless deep, the One who led His people through the wilderness to the Promised Land, and the One who did not abandon His people to exile in foreign lands, this One entered into our flesh to bear our sins and be our Savior. This Jesus encouraged us,

Fear not, little flock, for it is your Father's good pleasure to give you the kingdom. Sell your possessions, and give to the needy. Provide yourselves with moneybags that do not grow old, with a treasure in the heavens that does not fail, where no thief approaches and no moth destroys. For where your treasure is, there will your heart be also. (LUKE 12:32–34)

In this world, filled with adult challenges, it is so easy for us to lose sight of our true treasure. In our Baptism, by water and the Word, God made us part of His eternal family. This gift of eternal life is the greatest treasure we could ever receive, and it is ours as a gift. Jesus knew that the very world He created was corrupted by humanity's sin and would one day grow old and fail. Yet God's Word and promise would not fail. As we live in this world, God calls us to love and serve our neighbor. God has given us resources and responsibilities, and He has given us opportunities to care for others around us. As we do so, however, struggling against the ongoing brokenness of our sinful flesh and the corrupted world, we are to treasure what is most important. In Christ, we have an eternal treasure that will not pass away.

The River of Life

Read Revelation 22:1–5.

The Bible begins with Genesis and ends with Revelation. These two form the bookends of God's great plan of salvation. They focus us on not only what God has done for us but also what He has in store for us in the future.

In the original creation, in the Garden of Eden, God created all things out of nothing. He formed the watery deep into this world, ordering the chaos, separating the waters from the land and filling creation. At the pinnacle of that creation, God created people. God gave humans, made in His special image, the great gift of the tree of life. As they ate of it, they would live forever. Because of their sin in joining in Satan's rebellion against God, they were barred from eating of the tree of life. Just as they were exiled from the Garden, nourished by the rivers that fed the lush paradise designed for them, they were exiled from the tree of life that granted them physical immortality.

In Revelation, at the very end of the Bible, we catch a glimpse of the new creation. Jesus granted the apostle John a vision that included images recalling the Garden of Eden. He wrote,

Then the angel showed me the river of the water of life, bright as crystal, flowing from the throne of God and of the Lamb through the middle of the street of the city; also, on either side of the river, the tree of life with its twelve kinds of fruit, yielding its fruit each month. The leaves of the tree were for the healing of the nations. (REVELATION 22:1–2)

This vision depicts something even more grand than the original garden. There is a city and a river of life. The tree gives off twelve kinds of fruit, depicting wholeness and completeness not only for the twelve months of the year but also for the twelve tribes of Israel in the Old Testament and the twelve apostles in the New. At the heart of this new creation image is the throne of God and the Lamb.

The restoration of God's people to the new and greater creation at the end of time is only accomplished for us by the Lamb. This is Jesus Christ, the One promised to crush the power of Satan and restore God's creation. He suffered the very punishment of hell and death in the place of us sinful and undeserving creatures. Jesus Christ transformed the cross, the implement of His torture and execution, into a new tree of life. We, who are buried with Him and raised to new life in Baptism, who eat and drink His life-giving body and blood in the Sacrament of the Altar, and who hear and meditate on His Word, are granted access once again to paradise. Not by our own worth but solely by the work of the Lamb, Christ, who fulfilled God's plan of salvation and sits on His throne in heaven. God's people today marvel at this promise and at this hope, covered in Jesus' grace, and with John look forward to the day when,

> **No longer will there be anything accursed, but the throne of God and of the Lamb will be in it, and His servants will worship Him. They will see His face, and His name will be on their foreheads. And night will be no more. They will need no light of lamp or sun, for the Lord God will be their light, and they will reign forever and ever.** (Revelation 22:3–5)

Water from the Rock

During the time of Moses, some 1,500 years before Jesus, God freed His people from slavery in Egypt. God sent plagues of various sorts upon the Egyptian people, showing His superiority over the false gods of Egypt. God showed the powers of the world that He alone is the true God and all others are demonic imposters. The ten plagues ended with the Passover and the exodus through the Red Sea. These events, demonstrating God's liberation of His people from bondage, formed the nucleus of the nation of Israel. Their calendars oriented around recalling this event, and the recreation and remembrance of God's deliverance in the annual festival of Passover formed their identity as God's chosen and redeemed people.

Just as God's people were dependent on Him for rescue from slavery, they continued to be dependent on Him during their time of wilderness wanderings. The forty years of remaining in the wilderness, with the dry desert, harsh conditions, and encroaching enemies, refined and prepared this nation of freed slaves for God's purposes. Yet even though God provided miraculous daily food for them, protection for them, and victory over raiding enemies for them, they so easily forgot their dependence on God for all things. They grumbled, complained, and even rebelled against Moses. They questioned God's choices and Moses' leadership. They thought they knew better than God, and many of them suffered the just consequences for their rebellious thoughts, words, and actions.

Yet even in the midst of these sinful and selfish acts, God continued to care for His people. Though they thought themselves as in control of their lives and identities, they were dependent on God. In one stirring episode, after the people complained against God and Moses that they were dying of thirst, God commanded Moses to go to a prominent rock in the wilderness. There, the Lord revealed Himself before the rock. Moses struck the rock with his staff and water poured out, providing for God's people. It was as if God Himself were struck, and from His wounded side poured life-giving water for His people.

This highly symbolic act of self-sacrifice on behalf of an all-powerful God revealed to His people the great lengths He went to to provide for them, though they neither recognized nor deserved it. About 1,500 years later, the Son of God would sacrifice Himself on the cross for an undeserving and wicked world. In the meditations for this week, we look to how we, God's people, are dependent on Him, and how God is our rock in all of life's troubles. He provides for our needs of body and soul, and nourishes us by His life-giving Word like an oasis in a dry and thirsty wilderness.

God Is the Rock

Read 2 Samuel 22:1–4.

When you consider the biblical character David, what comes to mind? Chances are, if you know anything of David, you think of David and Goliath. This recalls the time when the shepherd David, too young to be an official soldier in the army of the king of Israel, volunteered to fight the mighty champion of the Philistines—and beat him in single combat. Sadly, the account of David and Goliath has become a cultural metaphor for scrappy upstarts taking on giant organizations. This is history; it happened. Through it all, David acknowledged that it was God who worked the victory against Goliath. God delivered His people and provided for them, and used the humble young man David as His instrument for delivering His people.

What is so often overlooked is that David's role did not end with battling Goliath. David was pursued by the vengeful king of Israel, had to survive off the land by living in caves, fought in many wars, and became king of Israel himself. As king, David's life was one of extreme highs and lows. God used him to win many battles against Israel's enemies, and David composed many psalms or songs of God's people that we still sing today. At the same time, David was guilty of great sins involving pride and lust, which led to the deaths of many, including an upright friend and his own infant child. David was betrayed by his friends and politically and militarily opposed for a time by one of his sons, before he was restored to power at a great price.

Near the end of his life, when he could fight no longer, David wrote one final song of praise to God. Reflecting back on his life, David wrote,

> **The Lord is my rock and my fortress and my deliverer, my God, my rock, in whom I take refuge, my shield, and the horn of my salvation, my stronghold and my refuge, my savior; You save me from violence. I call upon the Lord, who is worthy to be praised, and I am saved from my enemies.** (2 Samuel 22:1–4)

David was a great sinner who deserved nothing from God, either in life or in eternity. Yet David was a man after God's own heart. Through the trials of his tumultuous and eventful life, God always brought David back to recall God's faithfulness. In the song, David acknowledged that God was His rock and salvation, the one who saved David from his enemies by His mercy and grace alone.

Jesus Christ is the promised descendant of David—Jesus was often referred to as the Son of David during His ministry. David, however, was just a forerunner of Christ. God provided for David throughout his life; God the Father used Jesus to provide forgiveness, life, and salvation for this fallen world. God used David to defeat Goliath to save Israel. On the cross and in the empty tomb, Jesus defeated the ancient enemies of sin, death, and the devil to save God's people from their sins. David's God is our God, and He has done mighty things for us. In Christ, our God provides eternal deliverance for us. And just like He did with David, through His Word and promise of forgiveness, God brings us back to Him when we go astray.

Fed by the Word

Read Psalm 1.

The psalms made up the ancient songbook of God's people, but they are so much more. Inspired by the Holy Spirit, the psalms are instruction and summary. They are a guide for prayer, covering the whole scope of human emotion. They are prophecy, and no book is quoted more in the New Testament than the Book of Psalms. They paint a picture of life as God's people, hoping for and rooted in the promise of Christ.

Psalm 1, along with Psalm 2, makes up the introduction to this magnificent and varied text. In Psalm 1, we read about two ways: the way of the righteous and the way of the wicked. In this psalm, we catch a glimpse of what godly wisdom looks like and the destiny of the foolish who abandon that wisdom.

According to this psalm, what is the difference between the righteous and the wicked? The author states that the righteous person's

Delight is in the law of the Lord, and on His law he meditates day and night. (Psalm 1:2)

The word *law* in this context is broad. It refers to God's Word, what He has communicated through His prophets to His people. It is His teaching and His truth revealed to us. In other words, according to this psalm, the difference between one who is righteous and one who is wicked is that the righteous meditates on God's Word. The righteous person is one who hears, reads, or receives God's truth and is formed by it. The psalmist continues with writing that, for the righteous,

He is like a tree planted by streams of water that yields its fruit in its season, and its leaf does not wither. In all that he does he prospers. (PSALM 1:3)

God is the one who, through His Word, provides nourishment and growth for His people. God's Word is what makes us righteous as we are fed, formed, and transformed by it. And what is at the heart of this transforming Word? Jesus Christ. Later on in Scripture, John wrote that Jesus is the Word of God made flesh. In Christ, God has communicated His eternal epic truth that we are sinners in need of a savior and that God in Christ has restored us to Himself by the cross. All Scripture points us to Christ, and we who receive God's Word individually and in our worship communities are constantly fed by the Spirit, who continually forms and transforms us like a river that feeds and sustains a mighty tree.

The Christian life is one of living in the righteous identity that God has given to us in the Means of Grace. As those who have been made righteous by Christ, we are to continually abide in God's Word. Let us not consider this a burden, but rather a wonderful privilege and fundamental calling. When we read, meditate on, hear, and consider God's Word, the Bible, God provides for our spiritual needs like water to a tree, sustaining us for this life and the life to come.

The King and Princes

Read Isaiah 32:1–8.

Throughout the history of God's people, God sent many prophets. These served as mouthpieces of God, communicating His words and speaking His truth to their various contexts. Some spoke to everyday people, but most spoke to kings and rulers. God had appointed these kings, rulers, and priests to do His work for His people as they awaited the coming Messiah. God usually sent these prophets during times of upheaval for His people, calling on His people to repent of their sins and turn back to Him.

Isaiah was a prophet some seven hundred years before the birth of Jesus. He served as prophet over the span of four kings of Judah. During his ministry, Isaiah witnessed much. He, too, called God's people, especially the kings, to lives of repentance. He also saw God work wonders in destroying the army of the Assyrians. Today, Isaiah is most known by Christians for His prophecies about the coming Messiah. Few if any writers in the Old Testament compare to Isaiah's vivid prophecies that unfold who the Promised One from of old would be and what He would do. In one such instance, Isaiah prophesied,

> **Behold, a king will reign in righteousness, and princes will rule in justice. Each will be like a hiding place from the wind, a shelter from the storm, like streams of water in a dry place, like the shade of a great rock in a weary land.** (ISAIAH 32:1–2)

Though Isaiah spoke with many kings and rulers during his ministry, he knew there would be a greater king who would come after him. This king would not need any reproof or correction. He would not need prophets to speak God's truth to Him. Instead, this king would rule in righteousness. This king is Jesus. Through His cross and resurrection, He gives us His righteousness, that is, a right relationship with the Father forever. Just as God provided water through the rock in the wilderness, shelter for David in times of trouble, and nourishment for His people through the Word, King Jesus provides eternal protection and security for His people, just as Isaiah promised.

As for the princes in the prophecy, these are those whom God has called to care for us. God raised up prophets and priests in the Old Testament to enact His will and communicate His truth on His behalf to His people. Today, God raises up His people to do the same. He calls pastors to preach, teach, and care for His people, and parents and other authorities to do His work in the world. At the same time, He calls you in your various responsibilities to others to speak His truth through you. And through His Word and work in your life, others will receive His blessings now and in eternity.

Jesus Is Pierced

Read John 19:31–36.

The Bible is clearly not just a book. It is not just a collection of narratives or a selection of wise words. It is God's communication to us of His epic plan of salvation, and through it, the Spirit creates and sustains faith. God's Word, the Scriptures, point us to Jesus, constantly forming and transforming us to be more like Christ, the author and perfector of our faith.

As such, within the Bible there is a unity of purpose that God constantly unfolds and uncovers for us. As children, we can hear the Scriptures and understand who God is and what He has done. As we grow and continue, the more we read, meditate, and reread the Word of God, the more depth, detail, and nuance the Spirit uncovers for us. It is a limitless treasure trove of God's truth.

This week began with recalling the narrative of Moses and the rock in the wilderness. God's people were completely dependent on Him as they journeyed for a generation toward the Promised Land, and yet even when they grumbled against Him, God did not give up on them. He provided for them and their needs despite their selfishness and foolishness. God told Moses to strike a rock, and water came out to save the people from dying of thirst. The readings this week all point to how God provides security, safety, and salvation for His people.

In God's plan of salvation, in the unity of the purpose of Scripture, everything connects to Christ. He is the center. He is the climax of God's epic plan to restore this broken and fallen world back to God. As such, when we look at Jesus' crucifixion and resurrection, the heart of Scripture, we hear echoes from elsewhere in the Bible.

These echoes are not coincidental or made up. They are God's plan. After Jesus died on the cross for our sins, we read this seemingly insignificant detail,

> **But one of the soldiers pierced His side with a spear, and at once there came out blood and water.** (JOHN 19:34)

The connection is clear. What God did for His people in the wilderness through Moses was a foreshadowing of what He would one day do through the promised Messiah. Jesus was struck by the spear of a Roman soldier and out of His side flowed blood and water—pointing us toward His gifts of the Sacrament of the Altar and Baptism, by which we are saved. In His sacrifice, Jesus provided and still provides life-giving gifts to save and sustain God's people. Through the waters of Baptism, God grants forgiveness of sins; through the Sacrament of the Altar, God nourishes and sustains our faith for eternal life.

As we read and meditate on God's Word, we sit back and marvel at the unity of Scripture, how everything points us to God's saving plan for us in Christ. When we do, we are encouraged and blessed to recall how God always has and always will provide life for His people through Christ.

Jesus Is the Rock

〜〜〜〜〜

Read 1 Corinthians 10:1–5.

It is sometimes easy to fall into the temptation to believe that our lives are not connected to God's epic plan of salvation in Christ. We read the accounts of Scripture and compare those things to our own lives. It seems that the events of the Bible, from beginning to end, are dramatic and meaningful. Our lives, by contrast, feel routine and unspectacular.

When we turn to the Scriptures, however, we see a vastly different story about our involvement in God's plan of salvation. St. Paul wrote letters to the Church in Corinth that addressed their squabbles amongst one another and gross misunderstandings of God's truth. In the middle of one of these letters, he wrote,

> **For I do not want you to be unaware, brothers, that our fathers were all under the cloud, and all passed through the sea, and all were baptized into Moses in the cloud and in the sea, and all ate the same spiritual food, and all drank the same spiritual drink. For they drank from the spiritual Rock that followed them, and the Rock was Christ.** (1 CORINTHIANS 10:1–4)

In the midst of their petty debates, the people of Corinth were drawn back by Paul to recall God's plan of salvation, first through the rock in the wilderness and then through Christ. Paul is not necessarily saying that the rock Moses struck in the wilderness was really Jesus. Even though there were some Jewish traditions that pointed to this, Paul wasn't necessarily saying that a big rock dragged itself along behind the Israelites as they traveled through the wilderness.

Regardless of whether the rock Moses struck followed the people on their travels, Paul once again connected Jesus to how God provides for His people. The same God who stood by the rock and provided saving water for His people under Moses is the same God who was crucified for us and who continues to provide for us through His Means of Grace. This is our God, and this is not only what He has done for His people in the past but what He continues to do for us in the present.

When Paul mentions that the Rock that followed them in the wilderness was Christ, he is also reminding the people of Corinth—and by extension Christians today—that Jesus is with us as we journey through life. Jesus promised to be with us always, to the very end of the age. He sent the Spirit to be with the Church at Pentecost, and through the continued gifts of the Means of Grace that He delivers through the Church, the Spirit is still poured out on God's people today. He is our Rock, pouring out His mercy and grace to us as we gather in worship and as we gather to meditate on His Word in groups, in our households, and on our own in regular devotions.

He will never leave us or forsake us. He remains with us even though we do not deserve it. Connected to Christ, we are included and involved in God's epic plan of salvation just as much as any of those who have believed God's promises throughout time and space. God provides for us, just as He always has for His people, and in Jesus, we freely and joyfully receive God's living water even unto eternity.

Naaman Is Healed

Most of the narrative accounts in the Bible follow God's chosen people as the principal characters. At infrequent intervals, though, the perspective shifts away from Israel to other peoples and other nations. When Gentiles, or non-Jews, emerge as primary characters for a time in a narrative, we should pay special attention—God is doing something unique and powerful.

Naaman is one such example. Naaman lived during the dark days of the Northern Kingdom of Israel, when the kings had turned completely from worship of the true God to idolatry. But he was not an Israelite. Instead, he was the commander of the armies of the nation to the north of Israel, Syria. He also had leprosy, a devastating skin disease that always led to disfigurement and usually to death.

Israel and Syria had a tumultuous relationship, often engaging in wars and skirmishes with one another. In one such war, the Syrians raided and took some Israelites as slaves. One of the slaves that served the house of Naaman was an Israelite girl. She told Naaman, her captor, that there was a prophet in Israel who had the power to heal him. So Naaman, in conjunction with the king of Syria, sent a peacetime delegation to the king of Israel in Samaria with a bounty of treasure to pay the prophet of Israel to heal Naaman.

The wicked king of Israel thought the king of Syria insincere, looking for a way to entrap Israel in another war. So far gone was the unbelieving king of Israel that he did not even acknowledge that Israel had a faithful prophet, Elisha. Despite the king's unfaithfulness, when Elisha the prophet heard of this, he sent a request to the king to send Naaman to him. God would use this episode to show His power to heal and save His people despite the unfaithfulness of the king and the unbelief of the Gentile nations.

Naaman went to Elisha, and though he was reluctant to follow Elisha's instructions to wash himself in the Jordan River, he was healed of his leprosy when he obeyed the Lord's Word. God used the waters of the river and His Word not only to cleanse the Syrian general of his sickness but also to bring him to saving faith in the true God. Naaman returned to Syria, pledging to worship the God of Israel only. In this Gentile conversion, juxtaposed to the faithless Israelite king, we see not only how salvation comes by God's grace through faith alone but also how God desires that all nations would receive the Gospel, repent, and be forgiven.

This week, we will investigate Scripture passages and accounts that focus on God preparing us and cleansing us by water and the Word, with special attention to the Sacrament of Holy Baptism.

MONDAY

Crossing over the Jordan

Read Joshua 4:1–6.

Hundreds of years before Naaman, God's people were on the verge of finally crossing over into the Promised Land. Through Moses, God had miraculously brought His people out of slavery through the Red Sea, into the wilderness. An entire generation lived and died in that wilderness before God led them to the land He had promised to Abraham. Now only one barrier remained, crossing the Jordan River.

Though not as large a body of water as the Red Sea, the Jordan River made a substantial obstacle for God's people. It was not a massive river, but at the time of this reading, it was in flood stage. In addition, God's people were a mighty nation, prepared for war and conquest. We can only imagine the frustration God's people felt at being so close to their goal after waiting so long but also so far, given the raging river in their path.

At the river, God gave His people a command. This command defied logic and reason, and called upon God's leaders to trust His promise. Through Joshua, God commanded the bearers of the ark of the covenant, the traveling seat of God, to walk into the river. God promised that the river would separate for them so they would go through on dry ground. The bearers of the ark of the covenant obeyed, and God fulfilled His Word as He promised. The people passed through on dry ground, and at God's command, they made a memorial of stones in the river, and another along the bank of the river (Joshua 4:1–10). God commanded the people that, when future generations would look at the pile of twelve stones,

> **Then you shall tell them that the waters of the Jordan were cut off before the ark of the covenant of the LORD. When it passed over the Jordan, the waters of the Jordan were cut off. So these stone shall be to the people of Israel a memorial forever.** (JOSHUA 4:7)

Though this seems like a minor episode in the history of Israel, it has powerful implications for us as God's people today. The power of their entry into the Promised Land was God's Word. God commanded the priests to step into the Jordan River, and it parted for them. Without God's Word, His promise and command, the priests would have been swept away in the flood waters. God's Word made the difference between the expected and the miraculous, between exile and entrance, between life and death.

Holy Baptism works because God's Word works. Jesus commanded us to make disciples of all nations by baptizing and teaching. At Pentecost, Peter declared that Baptism forgives sins, and that this promise is for all people. In Romans, Paul declared that our Baptism is a Baptism into Jesus' death and resurrection, so that we who are baptized into Christ will pass through death into the new creation. In his first letter, Peter declared that Baptism saves us. God promises that the salvation Christ won for us on the cross and the empty tomb is attached to the water and Word in the Sacrament, and this is freely given to us. This is not a human act; it is a divine gift. Like with God's people crossing the Jordan, without God's Word and promise there would be no deliverance. With the Word, they entered into the Promised Land. With the Word of God attached to the waters of Baptism, we who are Baptized are made God's people. God promises us the blessings of entering the new promised land, the new creation, when Christ returns to make all things new.

God commanded the Israelites to make a pile of memorial stones in and alongside the river. When future generations saw it, they would be reminded of the power of God's Word to give them entrance into the Promised Land. When we look at crosses, we should be reminded of the power of God's Word to give us entrance to the promised land of the new creation through the life, death, and resurrection of Jesus, which we share with Him in Baptism.

Cleansing of Sin

Read Psalm 51.

There is a mutual understanding among people that, in order to make things right in your life you have to "clean up your act." In order to get into shape, you must clean up and change your habits and exercise. If you want better finances, you have to clean up your finances. If you want better relationships, you need to clean up your attitude toward yourself and others. To be fair, when it comes to so many earthly roles and responsibilities as human creatures, this has a ring of truth. God has given us various callings in life, and if we are to be faithful stewards of those responsibilities, we should be constantly examining our attitudes and behaviors, cleaning up those things that are detrimental, and acting intentionally and orderly.

But what about "cleaning up our act" when it comes to eternal things? What can we do to make things right in the spiritual realm? Is there anything we can work to do to "clean up our act" before God and make things right with Him?

In week 2, we considered the life of David. Besides being God's instrument to defeat Goliath and save God's people, David is also known for his horrendous sins of adultery and murder in the events surrounding Bathsheba. At the height of David's political power as king of Israel, he lusted after Bathsheba, another man's wife, and got her pregnant. David tried underhanded deception to cover up the affair, but to no avail. He then abused his political power to have Bathsheba's husband, Uriah, killed in battle as a way to cover up the affair. It would seem, from Scripture, that after these events David thought he had gotten away with murder.

God, however, knew what David had done. Through the prophet Nathan, God confronted David, exposing his terrible sin and calling him to repent. Crushed by God's good Law and justice, David was filled with great guilt. Though there were consequences for his sins, including the death of the child conceived in Bathsheba, God brought David to repentance and forgiveness. David wrote a song, Psalm 51, in response to God's confrontation. In it, David pleaded,

Have mercy on me, O God, according to Your steadfast love; according to Your abundant mercy blot out my transgressions. Wash me thoroughly from my iniquity, and cleanse me from my sin! (PSALM 51:1–2)

Did you notice David's wording here? David implored God to cleanse him of his sins—to give him forgiveness. This was not something that David could clean up himself. Sins against and before God cannot be remedied, fixed, or made right by our human force of will or action. Cleansing, or being made right, must come from God. Just like God forgave David of his sins, as undeserving as he was, God cleanses us undeserving humans of our sins by Christ.

In Holy Baptism, we are given that spiritual cleansing. Baptism is not an act that we perform to make ourselves feel better or to show how much faith we have. Baptism is a gift of God in which He truly washes away all of our sins, removing our transgressions and covering us with the righteousness of Christ. The entire life of the Christian afterward is living in that baptismal identity, regularly confessing our sins to God and being constantly and continually cleansed by His Word and promise. In that baptismal identity, God gives us strength and confidence to face each day as His people, striving to love and serve our neighbor as Christ loved and served us.

Fountain of Cleansing in Jesus

Read Zechariah 12:10–13:1.

When we consider the notable books of the Bible, it is unlikely that Zechariah makes any top-ten lists. Like many of the minor prophets, except Jonah, the content of these books is largely unknown to most Christians. This is a shame, as God spoke epic truth through these prophets to God's people during their lifetimes. Through them, the Spirit still speaks God's Word to us.

Zechariah was one of the last prophets of the Old Testament, and his book was written during a troubling time. Due to the people's persistent and ongoing sins during the time of the kings of Israel and Judah, God's wrath came down on His people like a hammer. The kingdom of Israel in the north was conquered, dissolved, and its people scattered throughout the Assyrian Empire. The kingdom of Judah to the south was later conquered as well, its cities leveled and many of its people exiled in Babylon. To the Jews who had experienced these terrible things, it seemed like God had abandoned them. They felt like God had given up on His pledge to restore creation to Himself in the Offspring He promised to Adam and Eve after the fall.

After seventy years, God handed the Babylonian Empire over to the Persians, and led Persian King Cyrus to issue a decree permitting the exiled Jews to return to rebuild the temple in Jerusalem. Work began, but when fierce opposition arose, the Jews halted the temple reconstruction and the site lay idle for years.

God raised up Zechariah (and Haggai) to prophesy in this context. Together, they persuaded the Jews to resume and complete the construction of the temple in which Jesus would appear. Included in this wonderful book, God through Zechariah looked to the future. He wrote,

> **And I will pour out on the house of David and the inhabitants of Jerusalem a spirit of grace and pleas for mercy, so that, when they look on Me, on Him whom they have pierced, they shall mourn for Him as one mourns for an only child, and weep bitterly over Him, as one weeps for a firstborn. . . . On that day there shall be a fountain opened for the house of David and the inhabitants of Jerusalem, to cleanse them from sin and uncleanness.** (ZECHARIAH 12:10; 13:1)

One thing unique about Zechariah is the detail God gave through him about the final week of Jesus' life (see Zechariah 11–13). In his prophecies, Zechariah conveys images and paints pictures of what Jesus would endure for the world. Jesus was betrayed by a disciple for thirty pieces of silver (Zechariah 11:12), abandoned by His friends, mocked and beaten, falsely condemned to death, and hung on the cross. There, those whom He loved watched as Jesus suffered and died for their sins. His side was pierced, and out of it flowed blood and water. By Jesus' suffering and death, His experience of God's wrath for all people for all time, we are cleansed and forgiven. Regardless of the sins of God's people during the time of the destruction of Jerusalem and their exile, God was still going to accomplish His plan of salvation. Regardless of our great sins today and the wrath we deserve, Jesus is still victorious over sin, death, and the devil. He is still cleansing our sins through His Means of Grace, and His gifts of forgiveness, life, and salvation flow for us like unending rivers in the wilderness.

Under the encouragement of the prophets Zechariah and Haggai, the Jews rebuilt the temple. God continued to provide for them through prudent leaders like Ezra and Nehemiah, and sent one final prophet, Malachi, to predict the coming of the Savior and lead the people by God's Word. There would be a period of time when there were no new prophets, but in the fullness of time, God sent His Son into the world to fulfill His promise. By His wounds, we are cleansed and healed in eternity.

Jesus Is Baptized

Read Matthew 3:13–17.

This week's readings focus on Baptism, and so it makes sense to also consider Jesus' Baptism. Jesus' Baptism, though, is unusual. Based on what we understand about Baptism, how through it God cleanses us from our sins and gives us forgiveness, it would seem that Jesus getting baptized would make no sense. In fact, when we really consider it, it would seem like Jesus would be the only person in the history of humanity who would not be baptized. After all, Jesus alone is perfect. When Jesus approached John the Baptist to get baptized, John thought the same thing. He said,

I need to be baptized by You, and do You come to me?
(MATTHEW 3:14)

Jesus' response, though, reveals so much. It reveals why Jesus needed to be baptized and what that means for God's epic plan of salvation. Jesus replied,

Let it be so now, for thus it is fitting for us to fulfill all righteousness. (MATTHEW 3:15)

Jesus' reason for being baptized is mind-blowing for us. Our Baptism is efficacious because Jesus was baptized. Jesus said it was right for Him to be baptized in order to fulfill all righteousness. In order to make a broken and sinful humanity right with God, to put us back in a reconciled relationship with Him after the fall into sin, something had to be done. Someone had to make things right. Jesus'

Baptism, then, was essential for making us all right again with God. How is this done?

Later in Scripture, Paul elaborates on the connection between Jesus' Baptism and God fulfilling His plan of salvation.

> **Do you not know that all of us who have been baptized into Christ Jesus were baptized into His death? We were buried therefore with Him by baptism into death, in order that, just as Christ was raised from the dead by the glory of the Father, we too might walk in newness of life.** (ROMANS 6:3–4)

Jesus' Baptism was the beginning of His ministry. From then on, He would journey for roughly three years, performing miracles and proclaiming the kingdom of God. As people were coming to John to be baptized, it was as if their sins were being washed away and left in that dirty water. They went in filthy with sin; they emerged cleansed by God. In the waters of His Baptism, Jesus took on the burden of the sins of the world. He alone entered the water pure and spotless before God. He emerged from that sin-stained water filthy with the corruption of our sins that He alone did not deserve. From there, He went to the cross. And when Jesus died and was buried, the sins of the world He took with Him were also buried. When He emerged to new life, He no longer had the filth of humanity's sins. They were left behind.

When we are baptized, Jesus takes away our sins. What He did on the cross and the empty tomb becomes ours in exchange. Jesus reaches through space and time to connect the waters of our Baptism with the waters of His Baptism. Jesus' Baptism changes everything for us, and in Him and by Him, we are cleansed of our sins and partake in Christ's victory over death.

Washed in the Name of Jesus

Read 1 Corinthians 6:9–11.

dentity is a huge topic in our culture. Who we are, how we identify ourselves, or how others identify us are all pressing concerns. The rise of social media has initiated a manipulated system of comparisons, built around automated algorithms to get the most "likes" and sell the most product. We are constantly comparing ourselves to others, making snap judgments, measuring our feelings of self-worth based on the filtered projections of others' life highlights. Add to that the sinful cultural obsessions with sexuality and gender identity, and the controversies regarding race and ethnicity, and the issue of personal identity gets even more complicated.

After Christ's victory over sin, death, and hell on the cross and in the empty tomb, He gave a mandate that as His people go out into the world, they were to make disciples of all nations by baptizing them in the name of the triune God and teaching them to obey His Word. As they went out into the world, either after Pentecost, due to persecution, or intentionally as missionaries, they established congregations all over the Roman Empire.

In one such congregation, established and nurtured by Paul, the Christian identity was put into question. In Corinth, not only were there false teachers who manipulated the Gospel message but there were also those who lived in open and unrepentant sin. Others in the congregation tolerated this wickedness in their midst. Paul, while he was separated from the Corinthian Christians, wrote two letters to them addressing what he had heard. In one letter, he wrote,

> **And such were some of you. But you were washed, you were sanctified, you were justified in the name of the Lord Jesus Christ and by the Spirit of our God.** (1 CORINTHIANS 6:11)

Paul reminded them of their identity in Christ. To be a Christian is not to conform to this world. This applied to the Christians in Corinth and also to us today. We have been given a new identity in Christ through the work of the Spirit. In Baptism, we have been washed of our sins and born again into the living hope of Christ. We have been connected eternally to the death and resurrection of Jesus Christ, and when we die, those of us who are baptized and believe in Christ will pass through death to the new creation. We have been sanctified, that is, made holy by the Spirit through the Means of Grace. As such, the Spirit not only has called us to faith but also still lives in us and works through us to produce good works. We have been justified in the name of Jesus, meaning we have been made right with God by the blood of Christ. Our identity is no longer our own; we are Christ's. We have been redeemed from the devil and restored to a right relationship with God through Him.

We rejoice in our Baptism. We rejoice that God has made us His own. We rejoice in this identity that trumps any other identity that culture or our selfish nature claims we should prize. We rejoice that we are in Christ, and He gives us the promise of everlasting life.

Jesus at the Well

~~~~~~~~

Throughout the different weeks in this Bible journey, we've considered different ways water contributed to God's plan of salvation, both physically and metaphorically. Of these, though, each week the focus has mostly been on how God provided for His people by giving water to them for their sustenance or applying water to them for their salvation. This week, we'll look at a different kind of water—living water that God puts inside His people.

In a notable and recognizable episode in Jesus' life, He and His disciples traveled through the region of Samaria. They stopped by a well, and Jesus sent His disciples to gather food. While He waited for them to return, a Samaritan woman walked toward the well to draw water. Jesus asked her, "Give Me a drink" (John 4:7). The discussion that ensued is fascinating as Jews and Samaritans generally hated each other, and men and women would not typically converse in situations like these. He knew her heart, however. He knew that the woman had been living in sin, thirsting for that thing that would satisfy the longings for her soul.

While at the well, using the imagery of their context, Jesus said that He could give her living water that would satisfy the thirst in her soul. The term "living water" indicates spring water. In areas of the world with few springs or rivers, people depend on cisterns to gather and collect rain water. Living water, far superior to cistern water, is always fresh and almost always abundant, bubbling from the ground to refresh and give life.

The living water Jesus referred to is the forgiveness and salvation He came to give to all people. The forgiveness that He gave, and the Holy Spirit who lives inside those whom God has called to Himself, is like living water, ever providing satisfaction for the true spiritual needs of God's people for eternity. The woman heard the Gospel and believed. Jesus used the location of the well to illustrate the biblical theme of the way God satisfies our spiritual thirst. This week, we'll investigate different passages that illustrate how God provides for our spiritual thirst through His Word and Sacraments and, as a result, makes springs of living water pour from us to others through His Spirit.

A Well in the Desert

Read Numbers 21:16–20.

It's easy for Christians to fall into the trap of expecting the spectacular. We all want our lives to be extraordinary, and we secretly hope and pray that God would provide signs and wonders for us at every turn. When confronted with difficult decisions, we pray that God would lead us in the "right" path, often seeking clear direction as options open up or close. Sometimes we feel at peace; other times we don't. It's easy for Christians to feel disappointed when we follow where we believe God is directing us and things don't turn out the way we want.

The reality is that much of our life as Christians feels, well, mundane and usual. We don't often experience what we believe to be spectacular things. Instead, we go about our days not noticing the great things God has done for us or has given to us. This is unfortunate.

In week 2 of this book, one of the prominent themes was the water from the rock. At the time of the wilderness wanderings of God's people, they were dependent on Him for everything. He provided food for them each day through the manna from heaven. The clothes and the shoes that they brought with them miraculously did not wear out over generations of use. He also provided water for them through a rock, a miraculous and spectacular event. Paul later connected that rock to Christ, the One who delivered them to the Promised Land.

As they get closer to the Promised Land, things change in the way God provides for them. Things get less dramatic and more usual. In the reading for today, God doesn't provide a sign for them when they grumble against Him. Instead, close to the Promised Land, God told Moses,

> **Gather the people together, so that I may give them water.**
> (NUMBERS 21:16)

Instead of giving water from a rock, God shows them a place to dig a natural well. To commemorate this, they sang a song,

> **Spring up, O well!—Sing to it!—the well that the princes made, that the nobles of the people dug, with the scepter and with their staffs.** (NUMBERS 21:17–18)

Notice the transition that happens here. God ceased providing for them through purely spectacular means and instead transitioned to more natural and expected means. The people, however, praised God for providing for them in this way. God's people knew that He was providing for them both in the miracles in the wilderness and in the well of living water at the border of the Promised Land.

God provides for our spiritual needs through His Word and Sacraments. He has given us His Spirit, who lives in us and works faith in us as we hear, listen, and meditate on God's Word. According to the world's standards, this looks rather mundane on the outside. Christians may be tempted to believe that if spectacular miracles and signs aren't happening in their life, then somehow their Christian discipleship is less epic or important to God. But like the Hebrews in the wilderness, we are to praise God for His gifts regardless of how much we feel we see God's direct hand in our lives.

In Jesus Christ, God has provided for our spiritual needs. He has given us forgiveness, life, and salvation. We receive these by faith in His promises through the power of the Spirit who lives in us. We cannot see Him, but the Spirit is present, constantly working faith in us through the Word like a well constantly providing fresh water at all times. And for this, we, too, can thank and praise God.

TUESDAY

The Soul Thirsts for God

Read Psalm 42.

t's easy to see pictures or watch videos of wild animals in nature and get a peaceful feeling. You've seen these before—a quiet stream in a forest with a mountain in the background. There are flowers in the field, majestic trees on the horizon. And there, a deer emerges from the forest, approaches the stream, and takes a drink. It all seems so serene.

In actuality, life for wild animals like deer is often difficult, dangerous, and short. In this fallen world, filled with danger and death, all of God's creatures struggle for survival against the elements and against potential predators. Wild animals are surrounded by disease and suffering, and finding food, shelter, and water in the wild is a challenge.

This is the picture the psalmist paints in Psalm 42, one of thirst and struggle:

As a deer pants for flowing streams, so pants my soul for You, O God. My soul thirsts for God, for the living God. When shall I come and appear before God? (PSALM 42:1–2)

The psalmist isn't painting a picture of the natural world, however. He's using this image to illustrate both our need for and God's means of achieving spiritual satisfaction.

In this broken and fallen world, we humans are all spiritually thirsty, whether or not we know it. We seek satisfaction for our souls in money, possessions, relationships, power, achievement, and other things. We are restless creatures, seeking a picture of the "good life" for our souls but always left unsatisfied and desiring more. Like a deer in a hostile world, surrounded by dangerous predators and a blazing sun, seeking out life-sustaining water, humanity fruitlessly searches for security, identity, and meaning in life. Apart from the true God, we are always unsatisfied and dead in our transgressions.

Yet God does provide for us in Jesus Christ. He is the means by which we not only know who God truly is but also receive life. By His sacrifice on the cross for us, He gives us the benefits of His life. By His thirst on the cross, suffering death and hell on our behalf, He satisfies our spiritual thirst for eternity. As He promised the Samaritan woman at the well, those who come to Him will receive living water that satisfies their thirsty soul forever. This is forgiveness and a proper restored relationship with God and the gift of eternal life.

In this light, as God's chosen and forgiven children in Christ, we pray that God would continually create in us a desire to return to the life-giving Word. We pray that God would remove any sinful barrier or bad habit that keeps us from receiving His gifts. We read the Word, we listen to it, we gather with other believers in the Divine Service, and we are nourished by the body and blood of Christ in the Sacrament of the Altar. And, surrounded by so much danger and temptation in this fallen world, our souls are satisfied by the gifts of the living God.

God, the Fountain of Living Waters

Read Jeremiah 2:9–13.

It's easy to take fresh water for granted. In an affluent society, in our homes, apartments, or places of employment, we can just turn on a tap and have clean, fresh water at our disposal. We can walk around public places and drink from clean water fountains. Beyond that, we have clean, fresh water in our tubs, showers, toilets, and dishwashers. We use clean water in our outside taps to hose down our cars or dirty sports equipment. Sure, we pay water bills for our water, but it's just something we consider an essential. In modern Western society, anyway, the water we draw is nearly always clean.

For most of the world, for most of time, this has been the exception more than the rule. Clean, fresh water is scarce. It naturally comes from springs deep underground or from fresh rain. Especially in areas where springs, streams, and rain are scarce, collection of rainwater for future use is necessary for survival. In the ancient world, rain was collected and stored in cisterns, containment vessels usually underground where rainwater could be stored for long periods of time. Unlike water from a spring, cistern water was dirty and stale, and cisterns could break or fail at different points. Clearly, spring water, known as living water, is most certainly preferred to stale cistern water.

During the time of Jeremiah, God used the comparison of living spring water and cistern water to illustrate the way His people had abandoned Him and looked in the wrong places for spiritual nourishment. He wrote,

> For My people have committed two evils: they have forsaken Me, the fountain of living waters, and hewed out cisterns for themselves, broken cisterns that can hold no water.
> (JEREMIAH 2:13)

In their time in exile, God's people had to face the consequences of their repeated rebellion against God. They endured much devastation and hardship. In this prophecy, Jeremiah likened their sin to abandoning fresh, clean, living spring water to drink dirty, broken-cistern water. They thought they did not need God and instead made idols they turned to for spiritual satisfaction. These false idols and ideologies did not work. They left God's people dying of spiritual thirst, destined to suffer the pains of hell due to their wickedness.

Yet God was still faithful to His people. Though they forsook Him, looking to replace Him and His truth with broken, worthless facsimiles, He brought them back to the Promised Land. Jesus called God's people to repent and believe the Gospel. By faith in Him, God's people now have the fountain of living water in them, an unending well of God's forgiveness, mercy, and grace. Through His suffering, death, and resurrection, this gift is now ours.

Like the people of Jeremiah's time, we are tempted by the devil, the world, and our own sinful flesh to abandon God and turn to other things to satisfy our spiritual thirst. When tempted, let us not give in but instead drink deeply of God's Word, by which the Spirit satisfies our souls for eternity.

Rivers of Living Water

Read John 7:37–39.

So far, in this week's meditations, we've focused on the use of the term "living water" in connection to the unending gift of mercy and grace Jesus gives us by the Spirit. By grace, through faith, we are granted the gift of eternal life. In another instance in Jesus' ministry, He added more nuance to this image and what that means for us. Jesus was in Jerusalem in the temple courts teaching,

> **On the last day of the feast, the great day, Jesus stood up and cried out, "If anyone thirsts, let Him come to me and drink. Whoever believes in Me, as the Scripture has said, 'Out of his heart will flow rivers of living water.'" Now this He said about the Spirit, whom those who believed in Him were to receive.** (JOHN 7:37–39)

How amazing is this! Earlier in the Book of John, Jesus had spoken to the woman at the well. He told her about the gift of living water He could give her. She believed Him and received eternal life. In this reading, we see Jesus some time later, standing up in the crowd. He declares to all that if they come to Him and believe that He is the Messiah, they would receive the Holy Spirit. Those who heard the Word of Christ and were brought to faith would be given that gift. What an incredible invitation; what an incredible proclamation of the Gospel by Christ Himself!

One thing that is so incredible about the way Jesus uses this image here is that He states that those who believe in Him and receive the Spirit would not only have a spring of living water but also a river of living water flowing out of their hearts. A spring or a well is usually localized. It gives a sustained but centralized amount of fresh water to a small region. A flowing river, however, has direction. A river is defined by its movement.

The gift of living water Jesus gives naturally leads us to movement. As those whom God has called to be His, given the benefits of the cross of Christ and promised eternal life, we are also called to speak God's truth. Like a river that flows to the sea, so the grace of God we've received by the Spirit flows from us to others. As we live in fellowship with other Christians and interact with unbelievers in the world, our words are to overflow with God's grace. In Christ, we, too, can echo Jesus' words to the world, "If anyone thirsts, let Him come to Christ and be satisfied."

Springs of Living Water

Read Revelation 7:13–17.

Try to imagine what life would be like if there was no concern about survival. Just try. Even in the relative comfort of the modern world, with technological advances and medicine, it's hard to imagine not worrying about survival. We have bills to pay, mouths to feed, jobs to work (or find), and people to care for. Every time we get in a car and rush down the highway, we know we're surrounded by risks and hazards. And no matter what we do to make our lives secure or mitigate risks, there's always the looming possibility of unknown diseases or cancer, which can appear at any time and upturn our whole lives. Concern about survival, and the struggle for survival, is central to every aspect of our lives, whether or not we're conscious about it. We have a hard time even imagining what life would be like without it.

Yet in the Book of Revelation, God paints for His people a picture of their future, where there will be no concern or struggle for survival. At the very end of the Bible, Jesus provided the apostle John with a vision of what life will be like in the new creation. In this vision, John recorded,

> Then one of the elders addressed me, saying, "Who are these, clothed in white robes, and from where have they come?" I said to him, "Sir, you know." And he said to me, "These are the

ones coming out of the great tribulation. They have washed their robes and made them white in the blood of the Lamb.

"Therefore they are before the throne of God, and serve Him day and night in His temple; and He who sits on the throne will shelter them with His presence. They shall hunger no more, neither thirst anymore; the sun shall not strike them, nor any scorching heat. For the Lamb in the midst of the throne will be their shepherd, and He will guide them to springs of living water, and God will wipe away every tear from their eyes." (REVELATION 7:13–17)

It's easy to miss this central theme of Scripture. God set out His great plan of salvation, even beginning to reveal it right after Adam and Eve rebelled in the Garden of Eden and brought sin and death into the world. The heart of God's plan was to restore humanity to Himself, culminating in the total undoing of death and the restoration of His creation to perfection. In this new creation, there will be no concern or struggle for survival, as God will satisfy every hunger and every thirst, both physically and spiritually. Jesus will be with us, wiping tears from our eyes and leading us to the never-ending joys and blessings of being God's renewed and refreshed children in paradise.

This is our future, won for us by the blood of Jesus Christ, which washes away our sins and makes us pure and holy before God. By the power of the Spirit working through the Word and the Sacraments, we have been given the gift of forgiveness and eternal life, satisfying the true thirst of our souls like living water in the desert. Even so, the joy we have now in Christ is incomparable to the future He has promised us. Then, there will be no struggle for survival, and all sad things will come untrue.

Jesus Washes the Disciples' Feet

This series is titled God's Living Water. So far in the main narratives for each week, we've focused mostly on the gift of God's salvation for us, focusing on how water is used or depicted in the Bible for our salvation. In this week's readings, we'll focus on another critical way Jesus used water to show us who He is and what it means to be His.

The night Jesus was betrayed, a lot happened. So much happened, in fact, that it's easy to forget how many events occurred in such a short time. The night began with Jesus and His disciples gathering together to celebrate the Passover. This is significant. The Passover was the central event in both the civil and spiritual calendars of the Jews. They remembered how God delivered them from slavery in Egypt, killing the firstborn of the Egyptians and sparing the firstborn of the Hebrews. Passover lambs were sacrificed, and their blood used as God's instrument to ward off death from their homes. This event kicked off a sequence of events where God brought His people through the waters of the Red Sea and eventually to the Promised Land.

Now, about 1,500 years after that first Passover event, Jesus and His disciples gathered to remember and to celebrate. Though His disciples did not know it, the next day, Jesus Himself would be sacrificed for the sins of the whole world. He would enact the final stage of what was foreshadowed in God's plan of salvation during that first Passover. His blood would be shed—and it would be the method by which God would deliver His people from eternal death.

Despite what was about to happen, Jesus' clueless disciples bickered at that final Passover. They argued over who was greatest, jockeying for position and prestige in what they misinterpreted was about to happen. Jesus' kingdom would not come in earthly political power but by His mercy and grace.

So Jesus set about doing the unthinkable to prepare them for what was about to happen. Even as His death was approaching, even as He anticipated suffering the pains of death and hell for this broken world, even as His followers argued over their importance, He stooped down and began to wash their feet. This was the job of a servant—a humiliating task: to clean the grime and filth His disciples had gathered walking the miles of dirty roads that day. Yet Jesus did it, showing His disciples that He came not to be served but to serve, and to give His life as a ransom for us. He also gave His followers an example. As Jesus served them, so they should serve their neighbors.

This week we will take a look at how God calls us, His people today, to love and serve our neighbor. As Jesus washed His disciples' feet, so we, too, who are baptized into Christ follow His example. By loving and serving our neighbor, sacrificing our own wants and desires for the good of others, we not only fulfill our purpose as God's creatures but also bear witness to the love Christ has for us to this broken world.

Love Your Neighbor as Yourself

〰️

Read Leviticus 19:9–18.

I f you've ever tried reading the Bible from cover to cover, starting in Genesis, it's likely that the Book of Leviticus has served as a kind of roadblock. The Book of Genesis reads like narrative, with many different interesting accounts. The first half of Exodus is written in narrative form, but the second half switches up the style by going into technical detail about the building of the tabernacle among other things. Leviticus can feel like a complete change of pace, and it's easy to get bogged down in the details. Why is that, and why does it matter?

Leviticus contains many of the laws and practices God expected of His Old Testament people. Through these laws, God taught Israel about how He shares His holiness with them and how they should live their lives in holiness. There are many details in the different ceremonial and civil laws that might seem strange to our ears. We are to remember that Jesus came to fulfill God's Law perfectly for us, and we are set free from the ceremonial and civil laws of the Old Testament. On the cross, Jesus made atonement for our sins as the final sacrifice for all people. After His ascension into heaven, Jesus appeared to Peter in a vision, signaling that many of the Levitical laws had fulfilled their purpose in preparing the world for His coming.

Leviticus, though, still has import for us today. Not only in it do we see God's plan of salvation revealed for us, but we also see how God wants us to love and serve our neighbor. Though the civil and ceremonial laws no longer apply to God's people like they did in the Old Testament, the Bible still teaches that God decides what is morally right and wrong. This applies to all people and is the ultimate truth. God has desires for how all human creatures live in relationship to one another. Nestled among the different laws of Leviticus, God included this:

> You shall not take vengeance or bear a grudge against the sons of your own people, but you shall love your neighbor as yourself: I am the LORD. (LEVITICUS 19:18)

Jesus in the New Testament affirms that this is indeed how God desires that His people live. Often called "the Golden Rule," this Old Testament teaching on how God would have us live was reinforced by Jesus. We are to truly love and serve our neighbor, sacrificing of ourselves for them and considering their needs above our own. But this loving service to our neighbor has nothing to do with us being righteous before God. On the cross, Jesus reconciled us to the Father, and by faith in Him, we are forgiven all our sins where we have failed to love God and our neighbor. Loving our neighbor as ourselves, instead, is God's desire and plan for us as His creatures.

As Jesus stooped down and washed His disciples' feet, this is what He was demonstrating. Whereas no disciple volunteered to do the humble task that night, Jesus showed what it meant to love His neighbor as Himself. Jesus then went to the cross to fulfill the sacrificial laws, sacrificing His life in exchange for ours. In Christ, we no longer follow the dietary restrictions, sacrificial codes, and other political laws like God's Old Testament people. But as He did for us, we are to still love and serve our neighbor, sacrificing of our own comfort and desires to truly love one another.

God's Care for the Needy

Read Psalm 9.

As you have read in previous weeks, David's life was full of good times and bad times. As a king, he knew what it was like to live in plenty. As a shepherd and a fugitive, he knew what it was like to live in danger and want. Having experienced these highs and lows, David wrote a psalm that included these words:

> **The LORD is a stronghold for the oppressed, a stronghold in times of trouble. And those who know Your name put their trust in You, for You, O LORD, have not forsaken those who seek You. Sing praises to the LORD, who sits enthroned in Zion! Tell among the peoples His deeds! For He who avenges blood is mindful of them; He does not forget the cry of the afflicted. Be gracious to me, O LORD! See my affliction from those who hate me, O You who lift me up from the gates of death.... For the needy shall not always be forgotten, and the hope of the poor shall not perish forever.** (PSALM 9:9–13, 18)

One of the most powerful things about the Psalms is that the writers understood the depths of the human experience. We all experience times, in various ways, when we feel abandoned and helpless. Maybe it's at home, at work, or in your finances. When David wrote Psalm 9, God was using him to declare His truth that God cares for the needy. Those who hope in God will not perish forever, they will not be forgotten, and they will not be abandoned.

As we return to meditating on Jesus washing His disciples' feet, we see an amazing contrast. On one hand, we have Jesus' followers, fighting over who would be the greatest. When Jesus told them that one of them, Judas, would betray Him, they did not understand. When He told them that they would all abandon Him that night, they all defiantly refused. Yet in the end, Jesus was right. He was betrayed by Judas, abandoned by those who claimed to love Him, and left to die alone. And on the other hand, we have the Son of God, stooping down to show His love for His disciples. The One who loved and served His friends willingly went to the cross for them. He chose to follow His Father's will. On the cross, Jesus was forsaken by His Father, experiencing God's wrath for the sins He didn't commit. He absorbed into Himself the very punishments of hell of those who forsook, denied, and abandoned Him. And He did all of this so that we, His people, would never be abandoned, forsaken, or denied by God.

Jesus washed the disciples' feet that night, knowing all that was ahead of Him. Yet He still did it, willingly, so that God's people would be covered in His mercy, grace, and forgiveness forever. He demonstrated in His own sacrifice the very truths that David wrote of in Psalm 9 a thousand years before. We who put our trust in Christ, who are brought to faith through the Spirit and the Word, will never be forgotten by God. In eternity, we will live in perfect community with Him. We who are poor and needy now, miserable sinners, who like the disciples betray and forsake God in our sins, are forgiven. Our need for forgiveness is achieved by His blood, and He is gracious and merciful to us now and forever.

The Suffering Servant

Read Isaiah 53:1–12.

As we considered in a previous reading, the prophet Isaiah lived roughly seven hundred years before Jesus was born. He ministered to four kings of Judah, and during his time of prophecy, the storm clouds were on the horizon. Isaiah began his time as prophet in relative peace but, near the end of his ministry, during the time of Hezekiah, Isaiah and God's people experienced great calamity. The Northern Kingdom of Israel was overrun, and Jerusalem was spared from utter destruction only by the direct intervention of God. King Hezekiah had been faithful to God, but his son Manasseh did wicked things. Tradition says Manasseh had Isaiah killed. In many ways, Isaiah's time as a prophet served as a transition point between relative security in the land of Judah and times of utter terror and desolation that followed.

In the midst of these drastic changes, where God's people were tempted away to worship false gods and were threatened by surrounding armies, God spoke epic words of prophecy. God spoke to His people, in powerful and clear words, about what the promised Messiah would do. In Isaiah 53, perhaps one of the most noted chapters of the Bible, Isaiah prophesied,

> Who has believed what he has heard from us? And to whom has the arm of the Lord been revealed? For He grew up before Him like a young plant, and like a root out of dry ground; He had no form or majesty that we should look at Him, and no beauty that we should desire Him. He was despised and

rejected by men, a Man of sorrows and acquainted with grief; and as one from whom men hide their faces He was despised, and we esteemed Him not. (ISAIAH 53:1–3)

The Messiah, long expected from the Garden of Eden and throughout the Old Testament, would not restore and save His people in an expected way. In fact, the prophecy foretells that God's people wouldn't recognize Him when He did come. Instead of welcoming Him and honoring Him, they would reject Him and despise Him. The prophecy continues,

Surely He has borne our griefs and carried our sorrows; yet we esteemed Him stricken, smitten by God, and afflicted. But He was pierced for our transgressions; He was crushed for our iniquities; upon Him was the chastisement that brought us peace, and with His wounds we are healed. All we like sheep have gone astray; we have turned—every one—to his own way; and the LORD has laid on Him the iniquity of us all. (vv. 4–6)

Just as the people of Judah and Jerusalem after Isaiah's time would turn from God to wickedness and unbelief, so would they turn from the Messiah and commit evils against Him. The One whom the people would not recognize and would reject would also be crushed. The very One who was long-expected and promised through the prophets would be pierced, chastised, and wounded. Yet at the same time, this torture and death would bring about peace between God and man. In the great mystery of God's mercy and grace, the very thing that sinners would use to bring death to the Messiah, the cross, would be the thing that would bring about eternal life for God's people. Like the sacrificial lamb in the temple or at the Passover celebration, the innocent, undeserving sacrifice would die in the place of and on behalf of guilty, deserving sinners. Isaiah then added,

Yet it was the will of the LORD to crush Him; He has put Him to grief; when His soul makes an offering for guilt, He shall see His offspring; He shall prolong His days; the will of the LORD shall prosper in His hand. Out of the anguish of His soul He shall see and be satisfied; by His knowledge shall

the righteous one, My servant, make many to be accounted righteous, and He shall bear their iniquities. (vv. 10–11)

The night before He was crucified, Jesus celebrated the Passover with His disciples. He bent down, wrapped a towel around Himself, and washed their feet. The Messiah, the Lord of Life, the King of kings, the Prince of Peace, chose to become a servant. The water He used to cleanse the feet of the undeserving disciples represents so much more than simple wash water. It represents the very reason Jesus came. He is the servant prophesied by Isaiah so long ago. He would not stop serving His disciples through kind acts; He would go to the cross to bear the punishment that they, and we, deserve for our sins.

With Isaiah, we marvel at God's goodness and mercy to us. We marvel at God's faithfulness to us despite the evils we commit. We marvel at Christ, the Suffering Servant, who died to cleanse us from our sins.

THURSDAY

Servant of All

~~~~~~

Read Matthew 20:26–28.

In psychology, it's still debated whether or not a "midlife crisis" is an actual stage people go through. Regardless of its scientific validity, it's part of our thinking in Western culture. In essence, the idea of having a midlife crisis involves getting halfway through your expected lifespan, looking back at what you have and haven't accomplished, and being filled with dread. As the popular stereotype goes, during a midlife crisis, people take risks, switch jobs, or start buying the things they always wanted in order to not miss out. With regrets about the past behind and fear of mortality ahead, someone having a midlife crisis, as it were, strives to live the rest of his or her life with greatness.

While Jesus' disciples were on their way to Jerusalem for that final Passover, they got into a sharp disagreement over who was the greatest among them. This argument, it seems, would continue even up to the Last Supper. As they argued about who was greatest among them, Jesus declared,

> **It shall not be so among you. But whoever would be great among you must be your servant, and whoever would be first among you must be your slave, even as the Son of Man came not to be served but to serve, and to give His life as a ransom for many.** (MATTHEW 20:26–28)

Jesus would later demonstrate what true greatness looks like when, at the Passover, He knelt down and washed the disciples' feet. Greatness in God's eyes is different from greatness in the world's eyes.

In the Garden of Eden, God created the first man and woman to love and serve one another, care for and cultivate His creation, and live in right relationship with Him. Service and love, as demonstrated by Jesus as He washed the disciples' feet, is why we humans were created. At the fall into sin, humanity became selfish and proud. Instead of looking out for the needs of others, we seek selfish gain, power, pleasure, and status. In our sin, we turn from God and from one another and deserve nothing but death and hell. Yet the Father sent His Son, Jesus, the sinless, perfect God-man, to do truly great things for us. He died on the cross for us selfish sinners, suffering for our sins and dying our death. In so doing, He opened the kingdom to all believers, giving His life as a ransom for many, just as He said.

As we are still sinners living in a broken world, we will still be tempted to seek worldly "greatness." At times, we will feel dissatisfied with our lot in life, regret past decisions, and fear death. In these times, we should remember our Baptism. The same Jesus who washed the disciples' feet was baptized to be your Savior. At your Baptism, God eternally connected you to Jesus' death and resurrection. Regardless of your failures, places you wish you had traveled but didn't, experiences you never experienced, or years you feel you've wasted, your future is assured. Jesus demonstrated true greatness by serving you, going to the cross to give you life. As you are in Christ, by grace through faith, His greatness is now yours. You will have an eternity with Him and all believers to live perfectly without regret. Until the new creation, follow Jesus' example by loving and serving your neighbor as Jesus has first loved and served you.

FRIDAY

God's Yes in Christ

Read 2 Corinthians 1:12–21.

For the final meditation this week, we look to the future. Throughout the readings for this week, we've focused on Jesus as our servant. As we are baptized, washed, and cleansed of our sins, we are in Christ. As Christ loved and served the world, going to the cross, we, too, love and serve our neighbor, following His example.

How does this identity we have in Christ, and the mandate to follow His example and love our neighbor, relate to our eternal future? This was a topic Paul brought up to the Corinthians, who had questions and concerns about "the day of our Lord Jesus," or Judgment Day.

> **For our boast is this, the testimony of our conscience, that we behaved in the world with simplicity and godly sincerity, not by earthly wisdom but by the grace of God, and supremely so toward you. For we are not writing to you anything other than what you read and understand and I hope you will fully understand—just as you did partially understand us—that on the day of our Lord Jesus you will boast of us as we will boast of you.** (2 CORINTHIANS 1:12–14)

This seems odd to us. Paul wrote that on Judgment Day, he will boast in the Corinthian Christians and the Corinthian Christians will boast of Paul. But wait a minute, isn't boasting bad? Isn't boasting prideful, and isn't pride sinful? Shouldn't we love and serve our neighbor in humility rather than have people boast over us? What does this have to do with Jesus' service?

For answers, we look to Judgment Day. On that final day, at the end of reality as we know it, Jesus will return as He promised. He will raise the dead, and those who believed in Him during life will be raised to the new creation. Those who did not believe during their lives will be cut off from Him forever. This is a hard reality. At the final judgment, as the last page of the chapter of God's plan of salvation comes to a close, there will be no second chances for those who were not believers in life.

But notice what is the difference between those who will rise to new life and those who will rise to eternal damnation. It's all about Christ. Jesus came not to be served like an earthly king or terrible warlord, but to serve and to give His life as a ransom for many. Those who will rise to new life will be those who, by grace through faith, are God's ransomed people in Christ. They will be those who have believed the promises of Jesus, received forgiveness, and been bought back from what they deserve in hell. Everything we have in eternity comes from Jesus. This applied to Paul, to the Corinthians, and to us. We can rejoice, be glad, be grateful, and yes even boast in the great gifts that God has given to all who receive them. That's why Paul continues,

> **The Son of God, Jesus Christ, whom we proclaimed among you . . . was not Yes and No, but in Him it is always Yes. For all the promises of God find their Yes in Him. That is why it is through Him that we utter our Amen to God for His glory. And it is God who establishes us with you in Christ, and has anointed us.** (2 CORINTHIANS 1:19–21)

At the end of all things, God's people will be together in the new creation forever. This only comes through Jesus, who fulfilled God's plan of salvation in us. We have no reason to doubt our salvation in Christ. If Jesus declares us forgiven, then God says yes to us on Judgment Day. He has done it. We can boast in what God has done for us, not because we deserve it but the opposite. Paul had great pride and joy in what God had done through Christ to the Corinthians. He told everyone about how Jesus had served and saved Him and others. The Corinthians could boast in Jesus' gift of salvation to Paul. We, too, marvel at what God has done for all those whom He has called to Himself. This is our new identity, children of God redeemed by Jesus, and we boldly share this. And when Jesus returns on the clouds of glory to make all things new, He who served us and gave Himself as a ransom for us will take us to be with Him in the new creation forever.

Thousands Believe in Jesus

Ten days after Jesus' ascension into heaven, something incredible happened. Like the end of one important chapter of a book and the beginning of another, God was at work in a special way amongst His people and in the world.

Jesus, during His time of ministry on earth, told His disciples that He was going to die, rise to new life, and then ascend into heaven. This ascending, going from the earth to the Father's side in the heavenly places, would be for their benefit. Why? Jesus explained,

> **Nevertheless, I tell you the truth: it is to your advantage that I go away, for if I do not go away, the Helper will not come to you. But if I go, I will send Him to you.** (JOHN 16:7)

Jesus promised that if He ascended to the Father's side, He would send His Church the Holy Spirit in a special way. In the divine mystery of the Trinity, Jesus would be with us always to the end of the age through the Holy Spirit. Jesus, in His glorified physical body at the right hand of the Father in heaven, would be with us all wherever the Spirit was. Jesus' work would be multiplied on earth, beyond the confines of space and time, through the Helper, who would work to bring many to faith through God's Word.

Jesus' promise came true. At Pentecost, the event ten days after Jesus ascended, He poured out the Holy Spirit on the believers in

Jerusalem. They spoke in many languages, boldly preaching Christ. Many heard and were brought to faith. They were baptized, and the New Testament Church was launched.

God has always desired that all would repent and come to the knowledge of the truth. His love for this fallen world is unending, and His desire is that the lost be found and the unbelieving come to faith. This week, we'll meditate on God's heart for redeeming the lost, which overflowed beyond the confines of His chosen people in the Old Testament to all nations. This overflowing living water, bubbling up like springs in the desert, is for all people of all times and all places, and gives eternal life.

That the World May Know

Read 1 Kings 8:41–43.

The geographical location of the Promised Land is fascinating. God promised the land to Abraham, some two thousand years before Jesus. God's people would not occupy the land God promised to Abraham for hundreds of years. Even so, God had picked out a very special place to settle His people.

Though not large in land area, the Promised Land (which now includes land in modern-day Israel) is unique. It is diverse geographically and ecologically. It includes plains, mountainous areas, coastline, rocky wilderness, fertile fields, and a geographical area with the lowest elevation on the planet (the area around the Dead Sea). It is also unique in its location in relation to international trade routes. Though on the continent of Asia, it is located on the north-south axis of trade between Africa and Europe. The Promised Land was literally at the crossroads of international travel and trade. People were always coming and going through the Promised Land, shipping trade goods, stopping at waypoints to rest, or bringing their armies.

One thousand years after Abraham, King David desired to build a temple to God in Jerusalem. David, as we've considered elsewhere in these meditations, was a man of war, so God did not permit him to build the temple. Instead, God promised David that his son would build the temple in times of peace. Thus Solomon built the temple to God in Jerusalem, and it was magnificent. It was built at great expense, with much ceremony and many sacrifices. At the temple's dedication, the cloud of the glory of the Lord filled the temple, showing God's special presence among His people and His blessing of the temple.

Amid all the ceremony, Solomon made a special prayer about one of the purposes of the temple. He prayed,

> Likewise, when a foreigner, who is not of Your people Israel, comes from a far country for Your name's sake (for they shall hear of Your great name and Your mighty hand, and of Your outstretched arm), when he comes and prays toward this house, hear in heaven Your dwelling place and do according to all for which the foreigner calls to You, in order that all the peoples of the earth may know Your name and fear You, as do Your people Israel, and that they may know that this house that I have built is called by Your name. (1 KINGS 8:41–43)

Solomon remembered that God had called Abraham out of the nations. There was nothing inherently special about Abraham or his offspring. Even so, God chose Abraham, gave him faith in His promise, and appointed him to a special role. Abraham and his descendants, including Solomon, were only God's people by God's mercy, grace, and choice. As was evidenced in Solomon's prayer at the dedication of the temple, God desires that all nations hear His Word, repent, and come to a knowledge of the truth.

As is evidenced in Solomon's prayer, the temple served as a beacon of God's truth to the many nations, tribes, and traders who traveled through the Promised Land. As they saw the temple, they marveled at the true God. Solomon prayed that, as they passed through the land, all would see the worship there, be convicted to fear the Lord, and come to a knowledge of the truth.

God has always desired that all nations, tribes, and peoples know and fear Him. He placed His people geographically in a region where God's Word could spread to the corners of the earth. Jesus would later sacrifice His life, die, and be raised to new life in the same city as that temple. He did so for the entire world, not just a select few. At Pentecost, the Spirit overflowed through those gathered there, next to that same temple, and those who left that gathering having faith in the true God returned to their nations. Then and now, God still desires that all people may know Him.

Declare God's Glory

Read Psalm 96.

One of the most consistent fears or phobias in adults is public speaking. For many, just the thought of getting up in front of a group and giving a speech evokes sheer terror. We do not like the idea of being unprepared or judged, of not coming across clearly or of messing up.

Related to this is talking to strangers. "Small talk" is a phrase used to describe what is culturally acceptable to talk about with strangers or during awkward silences. Small talk is confined to general-knowledge topics like weather and sports. Personal topics, related to politics or religion, are always out of the question for small talk.

What do the topics of public speaking or talking to strangers have to do with this week's meditation? At Pentecost, the Spirit rushed upon the believers, and they began to speak in foreign languages. They boldly, publicly declared their deepest beliefs about God. They relentlessly pursued reaching out to strangers and family members, proclaiming Christ and Him crucified. Though we read this extraordinary account and desire to follow their example of boldness in Christian witness, we need to be honest with ourselves. Most of the time, even considering following the example of the apostles fills us with dread and anxiety. Boldly proclaiming Christ in public, witnessing about our Christian faith? That seems too big a task for most of us, and so we easily fall into despair over our worth and ability as disciples of Christ.

David, some one thousand years before Jesus, offered us encouragement in our witness as God's people. In Psalm 96, he wrote,

Sing to the LORD, bless His name; tell of His salvation from day to day. Declare His glory among the nations, His marvelous works among all the peoples! For great is the LORD, and greatly to be praised; He is to be feared above all gods. For all the gods of the peoples are worthless idols, but the LORD made the heavens. (PSALM 96:2–5)

David was surrounded by enemy nations and tribes that hated God's people. Satan used the false religions of the surrounding nations and tribes to constantly tempt God's people away from the true God. David's life was not easy. Even so, David exclaimed that he and God's people should sing to the Lord, rejoice in His salvation.

Jesus is coming again, and all of creation waits for that day when death will die and life will reign under God's hand. Then He will restore each of His believers and His creation perfectly.

God's Desire That All Be Saved

Read Ezekiel 33:10–16.

One of the most frequent questions people have about God is why He would allow so many people to die in disbelief and be separated from Him forever. So many people, throughout time, have never had the opportunity to hear the Gospel of Jesus Christ and believe. Why does God allow this?

To answer this powerful and painful question, we turn away from asking *why* to asking *who*. Who is God? What is He like, and what has He done for us?

As we have explored elsewhere in this book, God's people asked the question of why God would allow such great suffering many times in their history. In one poignant time, roughly five hundred years before Jesus, God's people had turned their backs on the true God. As a consequence of their ongoing sin, God brought in the enemy armies of Babylon to conquer their cities and lead many of the people of Judah into exile. Even during this time, God sent prophets to speak His truth to His questioning and despairing people. Among so many other things, God gave this command to His people through the prophet Ezekiel,

> And you, son of man, say to the house of Israel, Thus have you said: "Surely our transgressions and our sins are upon us, and we rot away because of them. How then can we live?" Say to them, As I live, declares the Lord God, I have no pleasure

in the death of the wicked, but that the wicked turn from his way and live; turn back, turn back from your evil ways, for why will you die, O house of Israel? (EZEKIEL 33:10–11)

To the people in exile, God spoke that their suffering came from their transgressions. That was the answer to why this evil was happening. Yet God continued to explain who He is and what He desires. God added that He takes no pleasure in death, even the death of wicked sinners. He does not delight in pain and suffering. Instead, God delights when sinners turn from their sins and live. God does not take pleasure in the death of anyone. He wants all people of all times to repent and be brought back to Him.

Why so many die without believing in Jesus is not something God has specifically revealed to us. There are so many things God has not shown us in His Word, and so many other things we believe on faith. We just have to leave some unknowns in God's hands. What we do receive in God's Word, though, is a clear message of who God is and what we mean to Him. God does not desire that humans remain in suffering and death. So, in the fullness of time, God sent His Son to redeem us from our sins, overturn death for us on the cross and in the empty tomb, and call us back to faith in Him by the Word and Sacraments. When overwhelmed or burdened with that which we do not fully understand, or that which God has not fully revealed to us in His Word, we focus our eyes on Jesus and remember who He is and what He thinks of us.

Despite all that we do not fully understand, remembering what Jesus has done for us, we speak God's Word boldly to the world. We support the work of missionaries at home and abroad so more people may hear the Gospel and be brought to faith. We gather together with other Christians in worship to receive God's gifts and pray for those who do not yet have faith in Jesus. We join in our households and communities to study God's Word together so that more may be strengthened by God's Word in the Spirit. And we keep our eyes fixed on Jesus, looking for the time when all things will be made new.

Jesus Is the Way

Read John 14:1–6.

So far in this week's mediations, we've looked at God's overflowing grace, which He pours out on all nations and peoples who receive His Word and are brought to faith. Knowing who God is, it's easy to believe that God expects us to be overflowing in joy all the time. But what happens when our hearts are troubled? What do we do when we are upset and the overflowing joy of God's grace seems so distant?

The night of the Last Supper, Jesus taught many things. He demonstrated His love for His disciples by washing their feet. He gave them a new commandment to love one another. He also foretold that He would be denied and abandoned by His disciples. Jesus knew what was about to happen, that He would be abandoned by His friends, betrayed, and sentenced to suffer and die. And yet He thought of His disciples. He knew their hearts, what they were experiencing then and the guilt and shame they would experience after they abandoned Him. So Jesus prepared them with another teaching. He said,

Let not your hearts be troubled. Believe in God; believe also in Me. In My Father's house are many rooms. If it were not so, would I have told you that I go to prepare a place for you? And if I go and prepare a place for you, I will come again and will take you to Myself, that where I am you may be also. And you know the way to where I am going. (JOHN 14:1–4)

Knowing what would happen, Jesus assured them that what He would endure would be for their benefit. Though He would die for the sins of the world, suffering the punishment of death and hell for us, there would be more. He would rise again to new life and ascend into heaven. There, He would prepare a place for us. Jesus then assured them that He would return for us, to raise us from the dead and take us to the new creation He has prepared for us. We know from Scripture that those who die before Jesus returns will be with Him in paradise. When Jesus does return, though, He will take us to be with Him forever in the new creation, where our despair will be turned to joy, our doubt will be transformed into confidence, and our suffering will be turned to life.

The disciples were confused by this teaching, and so,

Thomas said to Him, "Lord, we do not know where You are going. How can we know the way?" Jesus said to him, "I am the way, and the truth, and the life. No one comes to the Father except through Me." (JOHN 14:5–6)

In these few simple words, Jesus taught His disciples, and continues to teach us, so much. To get to heaven and the new creation, we must go through Jesus. Despite so many false claims and teachings in the world, the way to eternal life is not through being good, being tolerant, or being accepting of all religions. The way to God is through Christ. And thanks be to God for that! Jesus has done all the work on the cross to forgive us our sins, and He has sent the Spirit through the Means of Grace to give us saving faith. He is at the right hand of the Father right now, and He is preparing a place for us in the new creation. He is the way to God, and we are His children by grace through faith.

Sometimes we may feel our joy in our faith is lacking. We may sometimes question whether we're being bold enough for God. In these times, remember that Jesus is the way. He's gone before us. In Him, we are given new life, not because of our overflowing happiness and joy, but rather despite our fears. And He is returning to make all things new and to bring us and all who believe to His side.

Proclaiming Christ

Read 1 Peter 4:7–11.

When teachers are beginning to put together a unit or course for instruction, they often follow the good rule of thumb of beginning with the end in mind. What this means is they won't have a clear idea of where they should lead their students unless they have a final destination in mind. For teachers, this usually means organizing things like course objectives, essential questions, and assessments. But how does this play out in discipleship? How do we keep the end in mind? What impact does that have on our daily journey through life? In his first letter, the apostle Peter gives us some wonderful encouragement:

> The end of all things is at hand; therefore be self-controlled and sober-minded for the sake of your prayers. Above all, keep loving one another earnestly, since love covers a multitude of sins. Show hospitality to one another without grumbling. As each has received a gift, use it to serve one another, as good stewards of God's varied grace: whoever speaks, as one who speaks oracles of God; whoever serves, as one who serves by the strength that God supplies—in order that in everything God may be glorified through Jesus Christ. To Him belong glory and dominion forever and ever. Amen. (1 PETER 4:7–11)

Peter encouraged His readers to keep a watch for the return of Jesus. He knew that, in the day-to-day routines of life, it is so easy to fall into the trap of thinking each day is just like the day before. Peter's teaching is that, in fact, each day could be our last! Jesus could return at any moment. If we lived like Jesus was likely to return and raise the dead at any moment, how would that change how we lived now?

Beginning with the end in mind means daily remembering what God has done for us in Jesus, repenting of our sins, and rejoicing in our identities as God's redeemed children. It also forces us to confront the reality that there is a hell. Those who have not heard the Gospel and who have not been brought to faith by the Spirit will not enter heaven. They will be cast out forever. This is sobering, and it calls us to action.

Peter commands His people to prepare for Jesus' coming. Keep watch and be self-controlled. Love one another wholeheartedly, forgiving one another. As we have been covered in Jesus' grace by the cross, so, too, do we love and forgive one another. As we forgive one another, the grace of Jesus covers all as well.

Included in the preparation is to be stewards of what we have and to show hospitality to one another. There is a world out there that does not believe in Jesus. So many people are lost, and God calls us to live as His people faithfully and joyfully, sharing the message of forgiveness and life in Jesus as we await His return. We have been emboldened and empowered by the Spirit, and the mercy and grace that overflowed to the crowds at Pentecost overflows to the world through the witness of Christ's Church. And if we live each day like it may be our last, then our last day will be like all of the rest. Amen. Come, Lord Jesus.

Lydia Hears God's Word

The previous six weeks of this book have focused your meditations on the different ways God's use of water in the Bible help Christians better understand God's great plan of salvation. From creation, to sustenance, to rescue, to life, water is connected to critical themes throughout Scripture.

This week, we mediate on a slightly different, yet related, theme. Paul and his missionary team (including Silas, Luke, and Timothy) were sent by the Church to bear witness to Christ to the ends of the earth. Sometimes they were warmly received by Christian brothers and sisters in the towns they entered; other times they were met with hostility. In Philippi, though, they were met with mostly silence. Philippi, a Roman settlement, had no synagogue. This meant that there were very few Jews in the area, as tradition suggested ten Jewish men were required to start a synagogue. As a synagogue was almost always both the first place the missionary team visited and also the basis for a church plant in that area, it would be understandable if Paul and his friends simply moved on.

The missionary team, however, did not move on to a new town with better prospects. Instead, they walked down to the river and found a few Jewish women gathered there to pray. Though a small gathering, Paul and the team proclaimed the Gospel to them. One woman, a merchant in wealthy goods named Lydia, heard the message and was brought to saving faith. She and her household were baptized, and the Church in Philippi was born. Though not explicit in the text, it is likely that Lydia's home formed the first house church, or congregation, in Philippi. Paul later wrote a powerful and joyful letter to the Philippians, one of the epistles in the Bible.

All this stemmed from the power of God's Word. In an unlikely place, with few prospects from a worldly standpoint, God brought sinners to saving faith. He used Paul and others to speak the truth of God's Word, and Lydia and her household were given eternal life. Through water and the Word, they were baptized into Christ's death and resurrection, and their eternal destination was forever changed.

This week, we will look at the power of God's Word in the lives of His people. The power of the Word does not come from us—our human power to persuade or to convince—but from the Spirit. As such, we, like Paul and others, can boldly speak the truth of God's Word and trust that it will work.

The Joy
of God's Word

Read Nehemiah 8:9–12.

Imagine living in a city with likeminded people but everyone outside the city in the neighboring towns and in the countryside hated you and the people of your city. You are cut off from other likeminded people, all of whom live hundreds of miles away. Also imagine that these neighbors were doing everything to undermine your city, including sowing lies and propaganda against your people and your God. How would it feel, and where would you find strength?

This is something like what God's people experienced during the time of Nehemiah, roughly five hundred years before Jesus. God had fulfilled His promise to return them to the Promised Land, and they returned from exile and resettled Jerusalem. They rebuilt the temple and worked to rebuild the city. Even so, the Jews were surrounded on all sides by neighboring tribes and peoples who did not want them there. They threatened the Jews in every way possible. The most damaging evil they had committed during this time was infecting the Jews with false worship. During the time before resettlement, the people who had remained in Jerusalem did not have the Word of God. They did not have copies of the Scriptures. And even after resettling, it seems clear that most of the Jews grew up with little to no exposure to the Word of God.

During this treacherous time, the governor, Nehemiah, and the priest, Ezra, worked reforms for God's people. They gathered the people of Jerusalem together and had the Torah, the Word of God, read out loud to them. Upon hearing what God expected of them in His Law, which they had not kept, the people of Jerusalem wept out loud in despair. But Scripture continues,

> **And Nehemiah, who was the governor, and Ezra the priest and scribe, and the Levites who taught the people said to all the people, "This day is holy to the Lord your God; do not mourn or weep." For all the people wept as they heard the words of the Law. Then he said to them, "Go your way. Eat the fat and drink sweet wine and send portions to anyone who has nothing ready, for this day is holy to our Lord. And do not be grieved, for the joy of the Lord is your strength." So the Levites calmed all the people, saying, "Be quiet, for this day is holy; do not be grieved." And all the people went their way to eat and drink and to send portions and to make great rejoicing, because they had understood the words that were declared to them.** (Nehemiah 8:9–12)

The message that the people had failed to live by God's command, the Law, had convicted the people to their hearts. Nehemiah, Ezra, and the Levites, however, knew the rest of Scripture as well. They commanded the weeping people of Jerusalem to go on their way and not to be grieved, as the joy of the Lord is their strength. They knew the Gospel, the good news that God does not and will never abandon them in their sin. This is the good news that, despite the rebellion and corruption of our sinful human nature, God offers forgiveness, life, and eternal salvation because of the cross of Christ. This is true joy in the Lord. This is God's plan of salvation, which has been accomplished for them and for us by Jesus Christ.

Just as He did with the Jews during the return from exile, God still uses the Law and the Gospel to convict us of our sins and point us to our Savior. The Word of the Lord shows us our need for God's forgiveness, which is a thirst that only He can satisfy. Through the Means of Grace delivered through Christ's Church, that same Word of God is living and active in the lives of God's people, forgiving sins and granting peace with God. It is all in God's hands, and God's Word gives life. This gives us great joy in the Lord. This is our strength.

Meditating on God's Word

Read Psalm 119:9–16.

Psalm 119 is an incredible section of Scripture. For one thing, it is the longest psalm, and by extension the longest single chapter in the Bible. It is made up of 176 verses and divided into twenty-two sections. Each section corresponds with a different letter of the Hebrew alphabet, and each set of eight verses within that section begins with the same letter of the Hebrew alphabet, corresponding to the letter for the section.

The psalm is also incredible for its depth in teaching God's people to meditate on God's Word. Psalm 119 identifies many different blessings we receive from studying God's Word, listening to God's Word, considering God's Word, and delighting in God's Word. In one notable section, the writer of the psalm asks,

> How can a young man keep his way pure? By guarding it according to Your word. With my whole heart I seek You; let me not wander from Your commandments! I have stored up Your word in my heart, that I might not sin against You. Blessed are You, O LORD; teach me Your statutes! With my lips I declare all the rules of Your mouth. In the way of Your testimonies I delight as much as in all riches. I will meditate on Your precepts and fix my eyes on Your ways. I will delight in Your statutes. I will not forget your word. (PSALM 119:9–16)

The word *meditate* has some curious connotations. Certain religions refer to mediation as an inward practice to gain enlightenment. This kind of meditation is not of God and should be avoided. Instead, we should heed the biblical view of meditation as outlined above. Meditation is not an inward reflection but instead a constant reflection upon something outside ourselves—the words and promises of God. This is what the psalmist would have us do.

The reality is that our corrupt, sinful nature does not know God or want to repent of our sins. Coupled with the temptations of the world and the railing assaults of Satan, we are hopelessly lost and condemned in our sins. That is, apart from God's intervention. In the fullness of time, God sent forth His Son into the world to redeem the world. Jesus came to deliver us from our sins, dying on the cross to give us forgiveness and rising to new life to give us eternal life. He came to overthrow the power of Satan. This all happened outside us and our power. God's gifts of forgiveness, life, and salvation through Christ are applied to us through the Word and Sacraments. They are not in you or because of you. They are for you because Christ came for you.

The same goes for the Word of God, the Scriptures. Though we are forgiven by Christ, our sinful flesh still continually tempts us to turn from God. When we study, reflect on, memorize and recall, listen to, or sing the Word of God, however, the Holy Spirit is at work. Like the psalmist wrote, as we meditate on God's Word, God teaches us the truth, helps us to avoid sins, keeps our ways pure, and gives us true delight. Let us store up the Word in our hearts, speak it, listen to it, and consider it in our daily lives, that the Spirit may continually work to give us joy and delight in our identities as God's forgiven people in Christ.

The Power of God's Word

Read Isaiah 55:1–13.

This week, we consider the great gift we have in God's Word. In the Old Testament, God spoke through the prophet Isaiah about so many things, including the coming of the Messiah. Isaiah prophesied about what would come to pass on the cross, as Jesus was the Suffering Servant for us all. But here, just a few chapters later, Isaiah prophesied again. This time, however, the prophecies speak to the New Testament reality of being God's people, redeemed and forgiven through Christ. And in this Easter reality, God proclaims,

> **Come, everyone who thirsts, come to the waters; and he who has no money come, buy and eat! Come, buy wine and milk without money and without price. Why do you spend your money for that which is not bread, and your labor for that which does not satisfy? Listen diligently to Me, and eat what is good, and delight yourselves in rich food.** (ISAIAH 55:1–2)

God invites all people to drink of the living water of forgiveness and grace, granted us through Jesus. This mercy and grace satisfy our souls for eternity, granting us eternal life. This offer, though, would not last forever, as God continued through Isaiah,

> **Seek the LORD while He may be found; call upon Him while He is near; let the wicked forsake his way, and the unrigh-teous man his thoughts; let him return to the LORD, that He**

may have compassion on him, and to our God, for He will abundantly pardon. For My thoughts are not your thoughts, neither are your ways My ways, declares the LORD. For as the heavens are higher than the earth, so are My ways higher than your ways and My thoughts than your thoughts. (ISAIAH 55:6–9)

It's easy to somehow think that reality as we know it will continue forever. This is true of believers and unbelievers, and we can slip into it without thinking. We go about our days, one after another. We work for the weekend or another break and then enter into the work cycle again. We plan for future events, and then even these come and go. But God calls us, as Easter people, redeemed by Christ and granted eternal life, to keep God's perspective of reality in mind. God's ways are not ours. God is God and we are not. There will be a time when reality as we know it will be over. Christ will return to judge the living and the dead, and there will be no second chances. Those of us who have faith in Christ will enter into the new creation. Those who do not have faith will enter into eternal damnation. And to this, Isaiah calls for all to repent. God does not desire that any should perish but that all would hear, repent, and come to a knowledge of the truth. There are unbelievers in our workplaces, in our communities, even in some of our households. To them, God calls for repentance. But He also offers this promise:

For as the rain and the snow come down from heaven and do not return there but water the earth, making it bring forth and sprout, giving seed to the sower and bread to the eater, so shall My word be that goes out from My mouth; it shall not return to Me empty, but it shall accomplish that which I purpose, and shall succeed in the thing for which I sent it. (ISAIAH 55:10–11)

God's Word has power. The Spirit uses the message of Law and Gospel to create and sustain faith. As we live in these times, waiting for the return of Christ and the end of reality as we know it, let us faithfully and joyfully receive this gift. Let us hear the Word, read the Word, and meditate on the Word wherever we are. Let us remember that God's Word accomplishes what He says it does: it creates and sustains faith. And as we do so, let us also boldly live and speak God's Word to those around us. Let us take our faith seriously, gathering together as God's people and devoting ourselves to the habits of abiding in God's Word in our thoughts, words, and actions. And in so doing, we trust that God's Word has power, and that God uses our witness and confession of the faith to draw more people to Him for eternity.

Treasuring God's Word

Read Matthew 6:19–24.

What do you treasure? I mean, what do you really treasure? What do you care for, why do you get up in the morning, what activities or things do you look forward to spending time with? There are, of course, cliché answers. We say we treasure our families, our work, our community, our churches. And it's certainly the case that you do treasure those things. You devote yourself to your responsibilities, and you work to love and care for those whom God has given you in your life: physically and relationally.

But when we look deeper inside ourselves, we see that we also treasure many other things. Of course, we treasure financial stability, our possessions, and our reputations. There are other things we treasure too. One of the best ways to know what things you treasure is to do a quick audit of your time. Apart from your livelihood and whatever else you do that you must, how do you spend your time? You likely spend a lot of time, hours a day, watching shows, scrolling on social media, or both at the same time. These likely signal that you treasure leisure or a sense of connectedness to the world.

But all these things we treasure, whether things deemed noble by the world or selfish, are temporary. One day, they will all pass away, fade away, or crumble to dust. Jesus spoke about this. He said,

Do not lay up for yourselves treasures on earth, where moth and rust destroy and where thieves break in and steal, but lay

up for yourselves treasures in heaven, where neither moth nor rust destroys and where thieves do not break in and steal. For where your treasure is, there your heart will be also. (MATTHEW 6:19–21)

Jesus entered into this broken world because He knew, in the corruption that sin and death brought, all earthly things would one day be destroyed. Even so, He put on human flesh to come and bear our sin and be our Savior. At His Baptism, He assumed all the sins of the world—He carried those to the cross and buried them in the tomb. At His resurrection, He rose to new life, having destroyed death by His death. Now those who are in Him have a new promise and a new hope. One day, Jesus will return, and those who believe in Him will have eternal life with Him. This is the greatest treasure of all. We have a treasure in Christ that will never fade away. Eternal life is the one gift that will not be destroyed.

So how then are we to live? We are to treasure His gifts: Word and Sacrament. We are to treasure the forgiveness that is ours; our everything depends on what Christ has given us on the cross. We have responsibilities here in life, and God gives us gifts and talents to use to love and serve our neighbor. As we value so much in life, though, let us not believe Satan's lie that the "good life" can be found here and now in possessions, relationships, or power. The true good life is waiting for us, and Jesus has gone ahead to prepare a place for us. God's Word is a great treasure we have now—for through it, God continually sets our hearts and minds away from the temporary things that are below to the eternal things that are above.

Equipped with God's Word

Read 2 Timothy 3:14–17.

t is fitting that we conclude this book and this series with a meditation on 2 Timothy. This book is usually regarded as Paul's last letter written before his death. He is in prison and seems to know his time to die is soon. He deals with familiar and heartbreaking feelings of isolation from his friends in prison, and he displays a special care for the church he knows he will soon leave. At certain points, the short letter reads a bit like a farewell address or a last will and testament.

Which leads us to Timothy. Timothy was a young man whom Paul met on one of his missionary journeys. Paul took Timothy under his wing, tutored him, and trained him for the pastoral office. Timothy was an invaluable companion and aid to Paul through his ministry. By the time this letter addressed to Timothy was written, Timothy was the pastor in the Church in Ephesus.

And what was Paul's specific encouragement and command to Timothy?

> But as for you, continue in what you have learned and have firmly believed, knowing from whom you learned it and how from childhood you have been acquainted with the sacred writings, which are able to make you wise for salvation through faith in Christ Jesus. All Scripture is breathed out by God and profitable for teaching, for reproof, for correction,

and for training in righteousness, that the man of God may be complete, equipped for every good work. (2 TIMOTHY 3:14–17)

Paul encouraged Timothy to cling to God's Word, to keep believing the Scriptures, continue studying it, learning more about it, and using it to teach, correct, train, and equip others. Even nearing the end of his life, Paul commended his dear friend and student to abide in God's Word. Of all the things he commanded this pastor, the next generation of Christian leaders, he strongly emphasized remaining in God's Word.

And that is our charge as well. The world promises so many things. Apart from Christ, they all lead ultimately to disappointment. Through it all, God's Word remains true. As we read the Scriptures, study them, meditate on them, and wrestle with them, God makes us wise for salvation. Our faith comes as a gift of the Spirit working through the Word, and as God's Word gives life, we are continually formed and transformed by it. That's why Paul commends Timothy to remember that Scripture does so many things, like teach us, correct us, and train us. As the Spirit does so, we are equipped for every good work God has prepared for us. Let us be lifelong learners of that Word, returning to the abundant waters of God's mercy and grace, being fed and sustained by the Spirit. As we live out our days as God's people, loving and serving our neighbor, we will also be looking to the horizon, waiting for the return of Christ, who makes all things new.